D1540987

New Approaches to Literacy

Helping Students Develop Reading and Writing Skills

Robert J. Marzano and Diane E. Paynter

PSYCHOLOGY IN THE CLASSROOM

A Series on Applied Educational Psychology

New Approaches to Literacy

Series Titles

*Becoming Reflective Students and Teachers With Portfolios
    and Authentic Assessment*—Paris & Ayres
Motivating Hard to Reach Students—McCombs & Pope
*New Approaches to Literacy: Helping Students Develop Reading
    and Writing Skills*—Marzano & Paynter

In Preparation

Assessing Critical Learning Outcomes—Berliner & Belshé
Building Home/School Relationships—Stiller & Turner
Designing Integrated Curricula—Jones, Rasmussen, & Lindberg
Effective Learning and Study Strategies—Weinstein & Hume
Positive Affective Climates—Mills & Timm
Positive Classroom Structures and Discipline—Ridley & Walther
Reducing Test Anxiety and Boredom—Tobias & Tobias

New Approaches to Literacy

Helping Students Develop

Reading and Writing Skills

Robert J. Marzano and Diane E. Paynter

AMERICAN PSYCHOLOGICAL ASSOCIATION | WASHINGTON, DC

Published by
American Psychological Association
750 First Street, NE
Washington, DC 20002

Copies may be ordered from
APA Order Department
P.O. Box 2710
Hyattsville, MD 20784

In the UK and Europe, copies may be ordered from
American Psychological Association
3 Henrietta Street
Covent Garden, London
WC2E 8LU England

Typeset in Berkeley and Arbitrary Sans by KINETIK Communication Graphics, Inc., Washington, DC

Printer: Braun-Brumfield, Inc., Ann Arbor, MI
Designer: KINETIK Communication Graphics, Inc., Washington, DC
Technical/Production Editor: Paula R. Bronstein

Library of Congress Cataloging-in-Publication Data
Marzano, Robert J.
    New approaches to literacy: helping students develop reading and writing skills / by Robert J. Marzano and Diane E. Paynter.
    p.   cm. — (Psychology in the classroom)
    ISBN 1-55798-249-X
    Includes bibliographical references (p.).
    1. Reading. 2. Reading, Psychology of. 3. English language—Composition and exercises—Psychological aspects. I. Paynter, Diane E. II. Title. III. Series.
    LB1050.2.M36 1994
    372.41—dc20   94-9054
                                                                        CIP

British Library Cataloguing-in-Publication Data
A CIP record is available from the British Library.

Printed in the United States of America
First Edition

CONTENTS

Teachers who attempt to enhance the reading and writing skills of their students face one of the most difficult tasks in education. Not only are reading and writing two of the most difficult processes to teach and reinforce but they are two of the most important. After working with literally thousands of teachers to improve their effectiveness at enhancing these key literacy skills and after surveying the research, we have come to some conclusions about how reading and writing can be taught and reinforced. We present what we have learned in this book.

Like most career educators, our beliefs and assumptions have changed over the years. We once conceived of literacy development as the acquisition of a set of discrete skills that are learned in a linear fashion. Although we still recognize the importance of specific skills, we now see that they are most efficiently acquired as a by-product of engagement in meaningful communication tasks. Ideally, while engaged in such tasks, the learner interacts with expert models (usually adults) who help them shape and sharpen their skills of literacy.

This new conception of literacy development has many implications for instruction. Fortunately, many of those implications are being implemented in beginning literacy instruction, primarily with reading and writing at the primary level. Unfortunately, those same implications have not, for the most part, been used in literacy instruction at the upper elementary, middle school, or high school levels. This book seeks to fill that void.

We caution the reader that the model presented in this book should be considered a starting point only. The teacher who wishes to use the research and theory on literacy development must be a student of that research and theory. However, we believe that we provide a sound foundation for such study. We also emphasize that we consider only two components of literacy development—reading and writing. Although they are certainly the cores of literacy, other processes such as speaking, listening, and viewing cannot be ignored in a comprehensive program of literacy development.

Robert J. Marzano
Diane E. Paynter

introduction

As described by the former Deputy Secretary of Education and former Chairperson and Chief Executive Officer of the Xerox Corporation, David Kearns (1985), "Literacy in its most basic form is simply the ability to read and write" (p. 3). Despite the fact that many popular books such as *Why Johnny Still Can't Read* (Flesch, 1981), *Cultural Literacy: What Every American Needs to Know* (Hirsch, 1987), and *The Closing of the American Mind* (Bloom, 1987) assert that literacy levels have dropped, the reading and writing competencies of U.S.

students are about the same as they were 20 years ago. (Mullis, Owen, & Phillips, 1990).

Although this might be interpreted by some as a reason for complacency about the effectiveness of reading and writing instruction in the United States, it is not. Rather, although the literacy levels of students have not dropped, the demand for literacy has increased. That is, to compete in today's world, U.S. workers must have higher literacy skills than their counterparts 20 years ago. Again, Kearns alerts us to the new demands on U.S. students:

> Literacy—real literacy—is the essential raw material of the information age. We are entering an era of lifelong learning that merges work and education .... We need workers who can adjust to change, who can absorb new ideas and share them easily with others. In short, we need people who have learned how to learn. (p. 3)

From the comments of Kearns, one can conclude that teachers must be more adept than ever at enhancing students' reading and writing abilities. Increasing one's effectiveness at reading and writing instruction demands an enhanced understanding of the processes of reading and writing. We begin by briefly considering two views of reading and writing instruction.

TWO VIEWS OF READING AND WRITING

Many educators believe that there are two very different, incompatible ways of approaching reading and writing instruction. In the following examples, one way is represented by Mr. Navarro's class, the other by Ms. Zimmer's class.

| EXAMPLE | MR. NAVARRO'S CLASS |

Students in Mr. Navarro's sixth-grade class have been reading books on the same theme—"families." Some of the poorer readers are reading books that were designed for third graders; some of the better readers are reading books that are intended for high school students. Mr. Navarro makes sure that students do a great deal of reading in his class. In fact, they spend at least 15 minutes of "quiet time" each day reading to themselves. Students also have a great deal of freedom concerning what they read. One day a student asked Mr. Navarro why he never has them do exercises in the reading workbooks like students in other classes. Mr. Navarro responded by saying, "You get better at reading by reading. We don't need the workbooks." The students also do a great deal of writing in Mr. Navarro's class. This writing is usually related to the reading they do. In fact, as students are reading their books on families, they are drafting their own short stories on the topic. By the time they are done reading their books, students will have completed their own stories. Some students have asked to read their stories aloud to the entire class; others are going to illustrate their stories.

| EXAMPLE | MS. ZIMMER'S CLASS |

Most of the sixth graders in Ms. Zimmer's class are working at their desks completing the seatwork that was assigned at the beginning of the period. At the beginning of the school year, Ms. Zimmer determined the specific strengths and weaknesses of each student relative to various reading and writing skills. Now students spend time working at their desks on exercises designed to enhance skills in areas in which they are deficient. When they are not working on skills, they are reading from a book that Ms. Zimmer has assigned. Each day they are responsible for reading a certain number of pages in the book. At least two or three times a week, the whole class discusses the pages in the book. Students are also working on a composition. The topic was assigned by Ms. Zimmer at the beginning of the week and is due in three weeks. Ms. Zimmer will read each composition, grade it, and return it to the student a few days after it has been handed in.

1 What do you see as similarities and differences between Mr. Navarro's class and Ms. Zimmer's class?

2 What would you identify as the strengths and weaknesses in each approach?

A NEW APPROACH TO LITERACY DEVELOPMENT

Although exaggerated to highlight the contrast, Mr. Navarro's and Ms. Zimmer's classes represent two very different ways of approaching reading and writing instruction. The story of the evolution of these approaches is the story of literacy development in the United States.

Reading and writing have always been considered basic to literacy development. In fact, less than two centuries ago formal education was organized around reading and writing. In the 1800s, Boston grammar schools were organized into two departments—reading and writing—each with its own master and two or three assistants. The reading and writing departments each enrolled students for half-day courses. Now, of course, we have greatly expanded our concept of literacy to include such elements as listening, speaking, and viewing, although reading and writing are still the core. Additionally, we have learned a great deal about the reading and writing processes—enough so that some people believe we can become much more efficient at enhancing the reading and writing abilities of students at all grade levels. We are among those who hold such a belief.

We believe that the information that current research and theory have disclosed about reading and writing can be used to greatly enhance classroom instruction. However, there is a price to pay for that enhancement. To use what current research and theory say about reading and writing, you first have to understand what this research and theory say about reading and writing. This book is designed to help you understand the new research and theory and to show you how to use that information in your classroom to enhance instruction. Finally, we hope to eradicate some of the myths about reading and writing that unfortunately still exist.

This book is designed to be used in a number of ways by teachers in pre-service and in-service situations. Specifically, the book might be used as a basic tool for self-study, as a manual for a training program, or as a supplemental text for a course on reading and writing instruction. We have included self-directed questions at the end of each goal to help you integrate what you have learned and apply it to your personal situation. You will also find that the suggested readings offer important supplemental information on key topics we have presented.

STATEMENT OF RATIONALE AND GOALS

The past few decades have witnessed geometric growth in our understanding of the reading and writing processes. This new understanding points to bold new approaches in reading and writing instruction. It also provides a framework in which two seemingly different approaches can be reconciled.

Goals

When you complete this book, you will have achieved the following goals:

1. An understanding of the two most popular approaches to reading and writing instruction and the perceived controversy surrounding them;

2. An understanding of the reading process along with knowledge of specific strategies for mediating the reading process;

3. An understanding of the writing process along with knowledge of specific strategies for mediating the writing process;

4. An understanding of the manner in which the two approaches to reading and writing can be integrated through mediated instruction.

goal one

Understanding Two Approaches
to Reading and Writing Instruction

Although the two approaches to teaching reading and writing illustrated by Mr. Navarro's and Ms. Zimmer's classes are sometimes described as being diametrically opposed, they are in fact quite compatible. However, before we discuss how they can be integrated, we first consider the two approaches separately.

THE SKILLS APPROACH

The approach we refer to as the *skills approach* is illustrated by Ms. Zimmer's class. The skills approach was developed as a result of a particular view of reading. David Pearson and Diane Stephens (1992) provided the following description of the perspective of reading that undergirds this approach:

In the mid 1960s, we tended to view reading as a pretty straightforward, perceptual process. Readers, we thought, accomplished their task by translating graphic symbols (letters) on a printed page into an oral code (sounds corresponding to those letters). After that, they "listened" to the sounds and to the words they had produced in the translation process. Comprehension of written material was nothing more than comprehension of speech produced by the reader. (p. 4)

In addition to the fact that reading was viewed as a translation process, the mechanics of that process were thought to progress from the smallest element to the largest element. That is, the skills approach assumes that the reader first focuses on translating letters, then letter patterns, then words, and so on. Phillip Gough (1972) described this basic process in his account of what happens during one second of reading:

1. The reader recognizes the bars, slits, edges, curves, angles and breaks in a letter.

2. The reader identifies the specific letter signified by the recognized bars, slits, edges, and so on.

3. The reader continues this process for all the letters in the specific word on which he or she is focusing.

4. The reader organizes the identified letters into a pattern.

5. The reader searches his or her lexical memory in an attempt to match the identified pattern with a known word.

6. When a match is made, the recognized word is placed in a semantic memory buffer.

For Gough, comprehension is a process of adding up the meaning of the pieces. As words are recognized, the meaning of phrases and sentences are gradually constructed. As more and more sentences are understood, the meaning of a paragraph is constructed, and so on. The central feature of this description of reading is that meaning is gradually built from the "bottom up." The reader begins with nothing and keeps adding pieces until he or she finally constructs the whole.

In keeping with this perspective, reading instruction is conceived of as facilitating the mastery of a set of discrete skills. First, the student masters one skill, then the student masters another. Of course, the skills that should be mastered first are those that relate directly to the first steps of the reading process: recognizing letters and letter/sound relationships. The list of skills to be mastered within a skills approach include the following:

◻ recognizing letters

◻ recognizing letter/sound relationships

◻ using phonics rules

◻ breaking words into syllables

◻ figuring out words from context

◻ figuring out words using word parts

◻ recognizing sentence patterns

◻ asking and answering literal questions

◻ asking and answering inferential questions

At one time, the ultimate expression of the skills approach to reading instruction was the basal reader. It is important to note that many of the basal readers on the market today have taken a much more integrated approach to literacy development than their predecessors. In fact, some of the basal readers used today incorporate many of the recommendations made in this book. However, in the early 1960s, virtually all basal readers ascribed to a sequential model of skill development. The characteristics of basal readers used in the 1960s were fairly uniform. Most included the following:

❑ a series of 15 or 16 books, several for each grade level (pre-primer, primer, and Grades 1 through 6)

❑ teachers' editions containing detailed lesson plans and instructions for teaching discrete reading skills

❑ soft-cover, expendable pupil workbooks containing exercises reinforcing the specific skills needed to use the reading books

❑ group-administered pupil tests to place students in the appropriate reader. If a test indicated that a pupil did not have specific skills, then that student was assigned to the reader and the workbook designed to teach and reinforce those skills.

Everything within a basal reader was coordinated to ensure the acquisition of specific reading skills in a specific order. The teacher's lesson plans focused on enhancing specific skills, the pupil workbooks provided practice in those specific skills, and the pupil tests were designed to determine whether students could move on to the next set of skills.

A basic tool of the basal approach was reading groups. Students were organized into homogeneous ability groups. All of those working on a certain set of skills and, consequently, a specific reader and its accompanying workbook were grouped together. Ideally, teachers had only three reading groups in their classroom: a high group, a medium group, and a low group. This allowed the teacher to interact directly with one group while the other two groups worked independently in their leveled workbooks. The pattern of interaction within a group might be described in the following way:

Teacher calls Group 3 to the front of the class. Children sit in assigned seats in a small group with teacher seated in the middle. Teacher says, "Okay, open your books to page 25. Rosa, begin reading." Rosa reads out loud and teacher interrupts frequently to make corrections in Rosa's oral reading ....

Teacher then reads comprehension question from the teacher's manual. Teacher calls on Anthony who is not paying attention ....

Teacher then asks child beside Rosa to read ....

After all children have finished reading, teacher begins the lesson in the skill that was the focus for that group and reads from the manual ....

On completion of that task, teacher says, "Okay, go back to your seats and do pages 32–34 in your workbooks."

Group 2 is called to the front of the class ....

In the 1960s, then, literacy instruction was organized around the systematic development of specific skills, and the task for teachers was clear: Develop specific literacy skills in a systematic fashion.

This bottom-up, skills-oriented approach to reading instruction persisted until about 1970, when two major publications caught the attention of educators.

THE WHOLE-LANGUAGE APPROACH

In 1967, Kenneth Goodman presented a paper at the annual meeting of the American Educational Research Association that drastically changed the perception of educators concerning the nature of the reading process and, consequently, the nature of literacy development. Instead of a precise process of using skills in a bottom-up fashion, Goodman characterized reading as a more imprecise, meaning-driven activity:

More simply stated, reading is a psycholinguistic guessing game. It involves an interaction between thought and language. Effective reading does not result from precise perception and identification of all elements, but from skill in selecting the fewest, most productive cues necessary to produce guesses which are right the first time. The ability to anticipate that which has not been seen, of course, is vital in reading, just as the ability to anticipate what has not yet been heard is vital in listening. (p. 2)

On the basis of this theory of reading as driven by meaning, Goodman hypothesized a very different reading process, which can be summarized in the following way:

1. The reader scans along a line of print from left to right and down the page, line by line.

2. He or she fixes at a point to permit eye focus. Some print is central in focus, some is peripheral, allowing the reader to consider single words or short phrases.

3. Guided by his or her knowledge of language, the type of text being read, and his or her understanding of the topic, the reader picks up semantic and graphic cues.

4. At this point the reader makes a guess or a tentative choice as to the meaning of the word or phrase.

5. The reader uses the representation of the text that he or she has already created to determine the reasonableness of his or her choice.

6. If the choice is acceptable, the reader forms expectations about the nature and meaning of the text that have not as yet been processed.

7. The cycle continues.

A comparison of this process with the one described by Gough (1972) discloses at least one major difference. Whereas the process described by Gough is a bottom-up one in which understanding is driven by recognition of the smallest parts first, the reading process described by Goodman is driven from the "top down." The reader's understanding of what will probably be in the text determines where he or she looks, what he or she looks for, and what he or she perceives.

Goodman, then, provided a different perspective of the reading process; Frank Smith (1982) provided a different perspective of the process of learning to read. David Pearson and Diane Stephens (1992) described Smith's contributions in the following way:

> Smith's revolutionary ideas were first presented in 1971 in a book entitled *Understanding Reading*. In this seminal text, Smith argued that reading was not something we were *taught*, but rather was something one *learned* to do. Smith believed that there were no special prerequisites to learning to read; indeed, that reading was simply making sense of one particular type of information in our environment. As such, reading was what one learned to do as a consequence of belonging to a literate society. One learned to read from reading. The implication, which Smith made explicit, was that the "function of teachers is not so much to teach reading as to help children read." (p. 8)

From the principles outlined by Smith (1982) and Goodman (1967), educators reasoned that reading and writing should be taught in a holistic manner as opposed to teaching specific skills in a linear fashion. In time, this general philosophy became known as the *whole-language approach*. It is the approach exemplified in Mr. Navarro's class. If you take a moment now to review the description of that class, you will notice that no skills were explicitly taught. Rather, the emphasis was on engaging students in the acts of reading and writing as much as possible.

Goodman (1986) outlined the basic tenets of whole language in his text *What's Whole in Whole Language?*:

> Language learning is easy when it's whole, real, and relevant; when it makes sense and is functional; when it's encountered in the context of its use; when the learner chooses to use it.
>
> Language is both personal and social. It's driven from inside the need to communicate and shaped from the outside toward the norms of the society. Kids are so good at learning language that they can even overcome counterproductive school programs.
>
> Language is learned as pupils learn *through* language and *about* language, all simultaneously in the context of authentic speech and literacy events. There is no sequence of skills in language development. Teaching kids about language will not facilitate their use of language. The notion that "first you learn to read and then you read to learn" is wrong. Both happen at the same time and support each other.
>
> Language development is empowering; the learner "owns" the process, makes the decisions about when to use it, what for and with what results. Literacy is empowering too, if the learner is in control of what's done with it.
>
> Language learning is learning how to mean—how to make sense of the world in the context of how our parents, families, and cultures make sense of it. Cognitive and linguistic development

are totally interdependent; thought depends on language and language depends on thought.

In a word, language development is a holistic personal social achievement. (p. 26)[1]

Since Goodman's description of whole language, there have been many translations and applications of his basic tenets, including those by Lucy Calkins (1986), Nancy Atwell (1987), Donald Graves (1983), and Jane Hansen (1987). However, all of them preserve the holistic nature of Goodman's philosophy.

HISTORICAL ROOTS OF THE CONTROVERSY

Although the skills/whole-language controversy came to the public eye in the late 1960s and early 1970s, it was actually the continuation of a much earlier debate, sometimes referred to as the *phonics/look–say debate*. In colonial times, reading instruction followed a very simple two-part process—teach children the code and then have them read. As Marilyn Adams (1990) explained, this translated into a fairly sequential form of instruction focusing on those skills necessary to break the code. Children were first taught the alphabet, then the sounds that corresponded to the alphabet, then strategies for attacking unknown words, and so on. Children then practiced these skills using materials that were read aloud. In short, the earliest form of reading instruction focused on the skills of decoding or phonics.

The type of materials students practiced on is worthy of note. Children were usually asked to read the Bible or patriotic essays. Their interest in the material was of little or no concern to teachers. Practicing the "code-breaking" skills was of prime importance. However, as educators began to consider seriously the importance of the search for meaning and its relationship to the reading process, they also began to question what children read. As Adams (1990) explained:

[1]Reprinted with permission of Scholastic Canada Ltd. Copyright 1986. Kenneth Goodman.

Those involved in education began to ask questions. If children are asked to read only materials for which they are intellectually ready, won't the meaning-bearing value of the text be self-evident? And if the mechanics of reading are properly subordinated to meaning from the beginning, won't the mechanics also be easier and more pleasant to master? But if students are immersed only in the "dull drill of practice" of letter-to-sound correspondence, won't they be deprived of—even, perhaps, permanently jaded against—the higher order mental activities of true reading? Indeed, given the seeming irregularity of English spelling, did instruction in letter-to-sound correspondence— or phonics, as it had come to be called— even make sense? (pp. 4–5)

Although this notion of "meaning-based" instruction was not as comprehensive as the whole-language approach described by Goodman (1986) and Smith (1982), it can be considered the precursor to the whole-language philosophy. Horace Mann, Secretary of the Massachusetts Board of Education, was the most visible proponent of this new meaning-based or "meaning-first" approach. He suggested that rather than learn phonics per se, students should learn to read whole words first (Balmuth, 1982).

By the 1920s, the meaning-first curriculum had gained a strong foothold in U.S. education primarily because literacy development was seen as the primary way of meeting the needs of a culturally mixed society: "The meaning-first curriculum was to foster the productive, creative, and responsible citizenry that emerges from knowledgeable and intellectually independent individuals" (Adams, 1990, p. 5). During the 1930s and 1940s, most major reading programs used a meaning-first approach in which children were taught to recognize whole words. If a word could not be recognized, context clues were used. Phonics, if taught at all, was used as a supplementary tool.

The whole-word or look–say approach met little challenge until the 1950s. In 1955, the publication of Rudoph Flesch's *Why Johnny Can't Read* changed the entire scene. Flesch argued that phonics instruction was the only sensible way of teaching beginning reading. The rationale underlying Flesch's argument was that a knowledge of phonics allows a reader to "sound out" any words that cannot be recognized on sight. In effect, phonics instruction provides students with a decoding tool that can be used in any situation.

Although the argument that Flesch (1955) put forth was quite sound from a learning perspective, Flesch went far beyond real teaching and learning issues. For him, the issue was a political one: "There is a connection between phonics and democracy—a fundamental connection. Equal opportunity for all is one of the inalienable rights and the word method interferes with that right" (p. 130). The connection that Flesch saw between phonics and democracy was a political one. In effect, he believed that attempts to suppress the teaching of phonics were motivated by a desire to keep the citizenry illiterate so that it could be easily controlled. This assumption made him no less than passionate about his convictions. Adams (1990) described the full force behind Flesch's efforts:

> Flesch did not confine his passion and politics to the issues at hand. He named names and pointed fingers. He called out the profit motive and impugned the intellect and honesty of experts, schools, and publishers. He developed conspiratorial motives, alluded to communists, and made insinuations about the intellectual predispositions and capabilities of females and minorities. (pp. 6–7)

Adams concluded that Flesch made an academic issue into a political and moral issue by blurring and suppressing the true nature of the debate. However,

Flesch's arguments were persuasive enough to shape the future direction of basal readers and to ensure their emphasis on phonics skills. This shift lasted until the 1970s. Unfortunately, the negativity spawned by Flesch has crept into the skills/whole-language debate of today even though the whole-language approach is qualitatively different from the look–say approach. As Adams (1990) noted, the skills/whole-language debate is commonly confused with the phonics/look–say debate:

> Today one cannot promote "whole language" instruction without having many perceive it as a thinly veiled push for "look–say" approaches to word recognition. To some, the very term "whole language" is translated to mean an uninformed and irresponsible effort to replace necessary instruction with "touchy-feely" classroom gratification—and worse. Similarly, the term "code-emphasis" is translated by others into an unenlightened commitment to unending drill and practice at the expense of the motivation and higher-order dimensions of text that make reading worthwhile—and worse. (p. 7)[2]

WHAT'S WRONG AND WHAT'S RIGHT ABOUT EACH APPROACH

As is the case with most situations in which two opposing sides are vehemently held, there is a bit of truth and a bit of error in both positions. In other words, neither the skills position nor the whole-language position is completely right or completely wrong. To illustrate, let's consider the skills approach first.

In spite of Smith's (1982) and Goodman's (1967) arguments to the contrary, the general processes of reading and writing are composed of identifiable skill components. In fact, much of the research on how the brain works indicates that it is much more compartmentalized than once thought. For example, Lynette Bradley (1983)

[2] All preceding text from Adams (1990) is reprinted with permission of the Center for the Study of Reading. Champaign, IL. Copyright 1990.

found that in the initial stages of learning to read, students use distinct visual, phonological, and motor strategies. Similar findings in the field of neurology have pointed to the "modular" nature of mental processes in general. For example, Michael Gazzaniga (1985), a researcher in the general functioning of the brain, asserted that the brain is composed of modular components:

> By modularity, I mean that the brain is organized into relatively independent functioning units that work in parallel. The mind is not an indivisible whole operating in a single way to solve all problems ... the vast and rich information impinging on our brains is broken into parts ... (p. 2)

So strong are the modular components in determining human behavior that Gazzaniga characterized the human mind as consisting of multiple but parallel "selves."

The major strength of the skills approach, then, is that it acknowledges the specific skills that are used in reading and writing. However, the major flaw of the skills approach is that it is based on the false assumption that because separate skills and subskills of reading and writing exist, they must be taught as independent entities. In fact, the opposite is true. Researchers in language development, such as Roger Brown (1970, 1973) and Carolyn Chomsky (1972), have established that learning the subskills and rules of language is best accomplished in a meaningful context. Children learn language by using it purposefully.

Of course, the major strength of the whole-language approach is its emphasis on purposeful learning. Whereas the skills approach seeks to develop specific skills, commonly at the expense of the authenticity of the learning situation, the whole-language approach emphasizes purposeful reading and writing. Unfortunately, however, the whole-language approach sometimes ignores skill development in the name of holistic learning. Without skill development, complex processes like reading and writing cannot be performed efficiently. In fact, some researchers assert that the skills of reading and writing must be learned to the level of automaticity. Researchers David LaBerge and Jay Samuels (1976) explained the necessity for automation using the analogy of basketball:

> In the skill of basketball, ball-handling by the experienced player is regarded as automatic. But ball-handling consists of subskills such as dribbling, passing, and catching, so each of these must be automatic and the transitions between them must be automatic as well. Therefore, when one describes a skill at the macro level as being automatic, it follows that the subskills at the micro level and their interrelations must be automatic. (p. 550)

Like basketball, reading and writing involve many skills and subskills, most of which must be executed automatically if the processes are to be performed smoothly and effectively. Not surprisingly, developing a skill or subskill to a level of automaticity requires a great deal of systematic practice.

In summary, learning complex processes like reading and writing requires the execution of specific skills and subskills at an automatic, even subconscious level. The whole-language approach makes no explicit provisions for the development of important skills and subskills, whereas the skills approach does. However, the whole-language approach does emphasize the critically important principle that learning skills should occur as a by-product of engagement in meaningful, realistic tasks.

INTEGRATING THE TWO APPROACHES

Because both the skills and whole-language approaches obviously have merit, it seems quite logical to integrate the two. From the previous discussions, we can conclude that an instructional scheme that emphasizes holistic tasks but that allows for emphasis on specific skills and subskills would preserve the strengths of the whole-language and skills approaches, respectively. Fortunately, there are theoretical bases for such an integration—one provided by Israeli psychologist Reuven Feuerstein (1980). In working with learning-disabled students, Feuerstein found that skill learning can be greatly enhanced if a skilled adult (a teacher) focuses on enhancing specific skills while a student is engaged in some task in which the skill is being used. Feuerstein (1980; Feuerstein, Rand, Hoffman, & Miller, 1980) referred to this as *mediated instruction*. Mediated instruction, as described by Feuerstein, is quite compatible with Russian psychologist Lev Vygotsky's (1962) concept of zone of proximal development. In simple terms, Vygotsky explained that skill development can be thought of as occurring in a zone. Within this zone of proximal development, the learner can execute some, but not all, skills independently. However, within the zone, those skills that cannot be executed independently can be performed with the aid of the teacher. Of course, the key component to such an approach is the teacher's ability to identify those skills that can be enhanced "with a little help." As Jane Hansen and Donald Graves (1992) noted, "Thus it is up to the adult to find out what the child needs and/or wants. This information is what is most learnable" (p. 814).

The key, then, to mediated instruction in reading and writing is a skilled teacher who can interact with students while they are reading and writing in such a way as to help them develop those skills that they cannot perform independently. This type of instruction incorporates the strengths of both the whole-language and skills approaches.

Such an instructional scheme has already met with great success for beginning literacy instruction. New Zealand researcher Marie Clay (1979) developed a model of beginning reading instruction based on teachers' observations of students' use of specific reading skills. When the teacher identifies a skill that can be enhanced, the teacher provides the necessary help. A key feature of this is that the help is provided while the student is engaged in reading. Clay's approach has met with incredible success with preschoolers and beginning readers. A description of Clay's (1991) approach to beginning reading can be found in her book *Becoming Literate: The Construction of Inner Control.*

Our book attempts to accomplish for reading and writing instruction at the upper elementary, junior high or middle school, and high school levels what Clay's system did for beginning reading instruction. Specifically, it is designed to provide a thorough understanding of two processes fundamental to literacy development—reading and writing—so that teachers can determine which skills can be enhanced through mediation.

SUMMARY

Whereas the skills approach emphasizes the various processing components important to reading and writing instruction, the holistic approach emphasizes the top–down direction of information flow of the processes and the context in which instruction should occur. Although there has been a controversy regarding the skills approach to reading and writing instruction versus a more holistic approach, the two are, in fact, quite compatible through mediated instruction.

Before beginning to examine the reading and writing processes, take time to reflect on this section and to answer the following questions:

1 Which approach—the skills or whole-language approach—most closely resembles your philosophy of reading and writing instruction? Describe the reasons you have adopted this philosophy.

2 Describe the basic theory behind mediated instruction.

ANSWERS TO QUESTIONS

We hope that your answer to Question 2 includes some of the following:

a. an emphasis on students learning specific skills while they are engaged in holistic tasks

b. providing aid for those skills that can be enhanced with a little help from the teacher

goal two

Understanding and Mediating

the Reading Process

Given that mediated instruction involves a teacher interacting with a student regarding specific components of the process being mediated—in this case reading—it is important that the teacher is knowledgeable about reading. In this section, we consider the reading process in depth. As we discuss each component of the reading process, we consider ways to increase students' skills and abilities through mediated instruction.

One of the basic conclusions of years of intense research is that reading is a very complex process. In fact, in the early 1900s, psychologist Edmund Huey (1915/1974) noted that to completely analyze what we do when we read would almost be the acme of a psychologist's achievement for it would be to describe very many of the most intricate workings of the human mind as well as to unravel the largest story of the most remarkable specific performance that civilization has learned in all its history. (p. 6)

In spite of its complexity, great advances have been made in our understanding of reading. In fact, in recent years some cognitive scientists—those who simulate human thoughts using computers—have been able to construct programs that, for all practical purposes, can read (see Just & Carpenter, 1987). These programs have

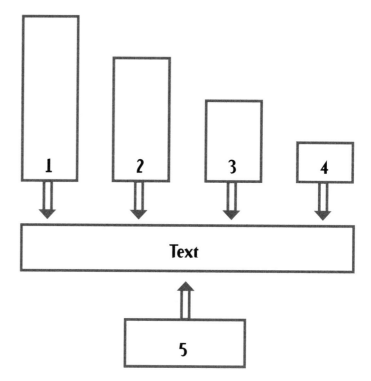

1. The general task processor
2. The information screener
3. The propositional network processor
4. The word processor
5. The macrostructures generator

Figure 1: *Processing components of reading*

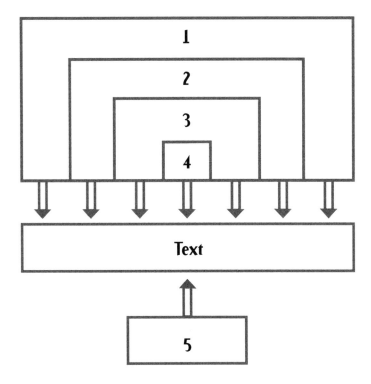

1. The general task processor
2. The information screener
3. The propositional network processor
4. The word processor
5. The macrostructures generator

Figure 2: *Alternate model of reading process components*

literally thousands of skill components. Fortunately, for the purpose of mediated instruction, we can use a much simpler model. In this text, we use a "parallel processing" model that we borrow from the field of cognitive science.

Parallel processing refers to the simultaneous execution of a number of separate, but interactive components. In our model of reading, we consider the five processing components depicted in Figure 1. The different sizes of the processing components shown in Figure 1 represent the fact that some processors are subordinate to others. Another representation of the interrelation among the five processors is shown in Figure 2. This figure illustrates that the word processor, for example, operates in the context of the propositional processor, which operates in the context of the information screener, and so on. One level passes on information to the levels below it. Additionally, the lower levels can pass on information to the higher levels. However, in general, the flow of information is from the top down. Remember that reading is a meaning-driven process. We consider each of the five processing components in depth.

THE GENERAL TASK PROCESSOR

The job of the general task processor is to monitor the extent to which the learner is getting closer to or further from some goal. This implies, of course, that effective reading involves the identification of a specific goal or purpose for reading. There are at least three major goals or purposes for reading that would be monitored by the general task processor.

One general goal is to simply enjoy an experience vicariously. This is particularly relevant when reading fiction. When you read Ernest Hemingway's *Old Man and the Sea*, for example, you vicariously experience what it is like to be an elderly fisherman battling a great fish. When you read Natalie Babbit's *Tuck Everlasting*, you vicariously experience what it might be like to live forever.

A second major goal of reading monitored by the general task processor is to gather information for a specific task. For example, if you are engaged in the task of researching the events that led up to the war in Vietnam, you would surely read selected books and articles on the topic. Your purpose in reading these books and articles would be to gather new information on these events. Similarly, if you were engaged in the task of buying a new car, you would read pamphlets and reports on the alternatives you were considering. Again, your purpose would be to gather information regarding those alternatives.

A third general goal is to affirm what you think you know. For example, while working on the research task about Vietnam, you might think that you know what happened immediately before President Johnson's decision to increase the number of U.S. troops in South Vietnam. However, given a desire to be accurate in reporting, you might conclude that you must check your facts and not rely solely on your recollection. You would again consult certain books and articles, but your purpose would be to verify what you know rather than to gather new information. This purpose would trigger a very different type of reading from that used when your purpose for reading was to gather new information or to enjoy experiences vicariously.

In summary, then, the three general purposes for reading that are meditated by the general task processor are to experience events and situations vicariously, to gather new information, and to validate what we know. Read the example below, and see if you can identify Alicia's general purpose for reading. After you have analyzed the example, read the discussion of it.

| EXAMPLE 1 | Last week Alicia's fourth-grade class went to the zoo. At first she wasn't very excited about the trip, but once there, she became very interested in the turtles she saw. The tour guide had mentioned that in many countries turtle soup was considered a delicacy and that turtle shells were frequently used for jewelry and decoration.

Alicia had never heard of turtle soup nor had she seen any jewelry made from turtle shells. While on the tour, she had many questions but never had any opportunities to ask the guide. When she returned home, she began searching through her books on animals to see if she could find out more about turtles.

| DISCUSSION | In this scenario, Alicia's purpose for reading was to gather information for a very specific task—finding the answers to her questions about turtles. It was this goal that led her to seek out more information about turtles.

Mediating the General Task Processor

Mediating the process of reading involves interacting with students in such a way as to provide help with specific processing components of reading *while* students are actually reading. That is, while students read, you provide help with the general task processor if it appears warranted or you provide help with the information screener if help is needed and so on. In this section, we consider ways in which you might help mediate the general task processing component of reading. Additionally, as we consider the other components of the reading process, we discuss how they might be enhanced through specific mediation techniques.

Problems within the general task processor occur when a student has not established a clear purpose for reading or when the student has not kept an established purpose in mind. Evidence that a student has not set a clear purpose for reading or has lost sight of the purpose is that the student has trouble attending to what he or she is trying to read. The student reads for a while, gazes out the window, doodles a bit, starts to read again, looks out the window again, and so on. Not surprisingly, when we lose sight of why we are engaged in an activity, we quickly lose interest in the activity.

Mediating the general task processor is fairly straightforward. It is a simple matter of bringing the student's purpose for reading to a conscious level. For example, you might ask the student, "What are you trying to accomplish by reading this book or this passage?" If the student has no clear purpose for reading ("I don't know, I'm just reading it"), then you can help him or her establish one. To help students set or clarify a purpose for reading, you might simply ask

❏ Are you reading this to enjoy it—to experience something new?

❏ Are you reading this to find some specific information?

◻ Are you reading this to check to see if you are accurate about something you think you know?

In addition to helping students clarify their purpose for reading, it is useful to provide them with strategies that they can use to accomplish the various purposes for reading. For example, if the purpose is to experience situations vicariously, then it is useful to continually relate what you are reading to your personal life. To illustrate, if you are reading *The Old Man and the Sea*, it is helpful to relate the experiences of the old fisherman to your own life. You can aid students in this aspect of processing by encouraging them to ask and answer questions such as

◻ Have I ever done anything like this?

◻ How were my experiences similar or different?

◻ Have I ever felt the same way as the characters I am reading about?

◻ How were my feelings similar or different?

◻ Have I ever thought in the manner in which the characters are thinking?

◻ How are my thoughts similar or different?

◻ Does this story help me understand something currently going on in my own life?

When your purpose for reading is to gather new information, it is commonly done for a specific task. That is, reading is being used as a tool to facilitate the accomplishment of some other goal. For example, if you are developing a report on the war in Vietnam, you will surely need to gather information. To accomplish your purpose in reading, you would continually ask yourself, "Is this information useful to my project about Vietnam?" When working with a student who has identified information gathering as his or her purpose for reading, you might facilitate the purpose by occasionally asking

☐ Is this information useful to you?

☐ Does this information meet some specific need related to your project?

A reader whose purpose is to verify what he or she knows about a topic will commonly scan a text very quickly looking for specific pieces of information. As the student does so, he or she continually asks, "Does this agree with or disagree with what I know about the topic?" When working with a student who has identified verification as his or her purpose, you can facilitate general task processing by asking questions such as,

☐ Which information disagrees with or contradicts what you understand about the topic?

☐ Which information agrees with or supports what you know about the topic?

In general, then, mediating the general task processing component of reading is a matter of helping the reader identify a specific purpose for reading or helping the reader focus on a purpose that has been previously established. Once a purpose has been made salient, controlling for that purpose can be facilitated by systematically asking and answering specific questions.

THE GENERAL INFORMATION SCREENER

While reading, the learner is constantly making decisions about the information contained in the text. In effect, the reader is screening information as he or she reads to determine whether it is reasonable—whether it should be accepted without further review or whether it should be rejected. If information is judged to be reasonable, it is integrated into the learner's existing knowledge base. However, if the information is judged to be unreasonable, then it is processed in a very different way.

To illustrate how the general information screener works, imagine that you are reading a book about the war in Vietnam—a topic you have been interested in for quite some time. As you read the book, you might run across certain facts that "don't seem right"—they might even contradict what you think you know about Vietnam. In such cases, you would look to see if evidence was provided. ("Where's the proof for this?") If evidence was not provided, you would refrain from accepting the information as true. ("I don't believe this even if the book says so.") If evidence was provided, you would make a determination as to the sufficiency of that evidence. Again, if you concluded that the evidence was not adequate, you would refrain from integrating it into your knowledge base. However, if you determined that the evidence was sufficient, then the information would be considered a legitimate addition to what you already know about the topic. ("I guess I was wrong. It must have happened the way the book says.")

In summary, the information screener determines the reasonableness of information given the current knowledge base of the reader. The reader goes through a process of analyzing the strength of the evidence presented for the information and either rejects or accepts the information based on the analysis. If the reader accepts the information, he or she integrates it with his or her existing knowledge. Read Example 2 about Alicia and see if you can observe the general information screener at work.

| EXAMPLE 2 | While looking through her books, Alicia found a passage in the encyclopedia that stated that turtle soup is a delicacy found in very exclusive and expensive restaurants. It also mentioned that turtle shells are imported into the United States in great numbers and that these shells are used to make earrings and necklaces as well as other decorative items.

Not all of this seemed correct to Alicia. She thought that turtle soup might be found in exclusive restaurants but remembered seeing a program on TV that reported that certain animal coverings could not legally be brought into the United States. She thought that turtle shells might be one of these forbidden imports. Alicia decided to check when the encyclopedia she was using was published, only to discover that the information was not very current.

DISCUSSION In this scenario, Alicia screened the information that she read in the encyclopedia. Her prior knowledge alerted her to the fact that some of the information might not be true although some of it seemed to be in line with what she already knew. Because the information she received about turtle soup made sense to her, she accepted it. She knew that expensive restaurants served very different and interesting specialty dishes. The information regarding the importing of turtle shells, however, did not seem reasonable given her prior knowledge; therefore, she looked for evidence that would validate or negate it.

Mediating the Information Screener

Evidence that a reader is experiencing difficulties with the general information screener is that he or she cannot describe whether the information being read seems reasonable. For example, if you ask a student to comment on the reasonableness of what he or she is reading and the student cannot answer ("I'm not sure if it makes sense") or does not understand what you are asking ("Huh?"), it is probably an indication that he or she is having difficulty at the information screening level.

A helpful mediation technique is to provide students with a specific strategy to increase their awareness of the necessity to screen information. One such strategy involves the following steps:

1. Ask yourself, "Does this information make sense to me based on what I know about the topic?" If yes, then keep on reading.

2. If no, ask yourself, "Does the author provide evidence for the information that does not seem reasonable to me?"

3. If no, then refrain from accepting the information as valid.

4. If yes, then try to determine how sound the evidence is.

5. If the evidence provided is sound, then accept it as new information about the topic.

6. If the evidence provided is not sound, then do not accept the new information until better evidence is provided.

This process is presented in flow chart form in Figure 3.

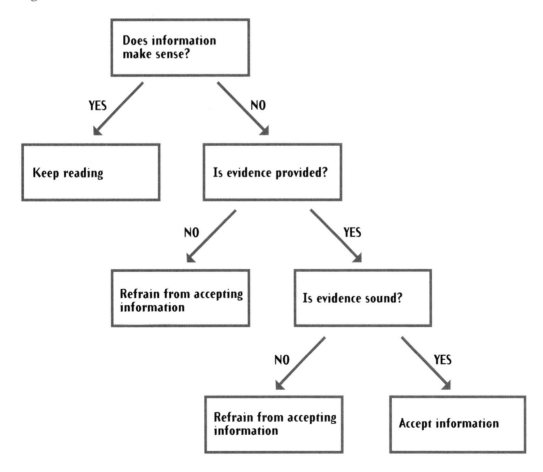

Figure 3: *Information screening strategy*

Logical Errors

To use this strategy, a student must understand some basic principles about sound evidence. Fortunately, research and theory by individuals such as Stephen Toulmin and his colleagues (Toulmin, 1958; Toulmin, Rieke, & Janik, 1981) have identified common errors that render evidence unsound. We have grouped these errors into three basic categories:

Category I: Errors Based on Faulty Logic
Errors that fall into this category use a type of reasoning that is flawed in some way or is simply not rigorous. Such errors include

a. *Contradiction.* The writer or speaker presents information that is in direct opposition to other information within the same argument.

b. *Accident.* The writer or speaker fails to recognize that an argument is based on an exception to a rule.

c. *False cause.* The writer or speaker confuses a temporal order of events with causality or oversimplifies a complex causal network.

d. *Begging the question (circularity).* The writer or speaker makes a claim and then argues for it by advancing grounds with meaning simply equivalent to that of the original claim.

e. *Evading the issue.* The writer or speaker sidesteps an issue by changing the topic.

f. *Arguing from ignorance.* The writer or speaker argues that a claim is justified simply because its opposite cannot be proved.

g. *Composition and division.* Composition involves the writer or speaker asserting about a whole something that is true of its parts. Division involves asserting about the parts something that is true of the whole.

Category II: Errors Based on Attack
Informal fallacies in this category all use the strategy of attacking a person or position.

a. *Poisoning the well.* The writer or speaker is committed to his or her position to such a degree that he or she explains away absolutely everything that others offer in opposition to this position.

b. *Arguing against the person.* The writer or speaker rejects a claim on the basis of derogatory facts (real or alleged) about the person making the claim.

c. *Appealing to force.* The writer or speaker uses threats to establish the validity of a claim.

Category III: Errors Based on Weak References
In these informal fallacies, the writer or speaker appeals to something other than reason to make his or her point; however, the appeals are not based on attack against a person or idea.

a. *Appealing to authority.* The writer or speaker evokes authority as the last word on an issue.

b. *Appealing to the people.* The writer or speaker attempts to justify a claim on the basis of popularity.

c. *Appealing to emotion.* The writer or speaker uses an emotion-laden or "sob" story as proof for a claim.

Of course, you cannot expect students to understand and learn all of these types of fallacies at once. However, if students are introduced to one or more at systematic intervals, they quickly develop an impressive understanding of common fallacies. In the last section of this book, we describe how to teach students about the three categories of informal fallacies as well as cover other information related to the reading process. For now, assume that you have exposed students to some of these common errors. When mediating the reading process to enhance the information screener, you might orally guide students through the strategy depicted in Figure 3. That is, you would walk students through the various questions within the process: "Does this information make sense to you based on what you know about the topic?", "If not, does the writer provide evidence …?", and so on. When students are addressing the question regarding evidence, you would then consider the various types of errors that render evidence invalid. For example, you might ask students questions such as

❑ Do you notice any contradictions in the evidence that has been provided?

❑ Do you notice that the writer's evidence is based on an exception to the rule?

❑ Do you notice that the writer has made the error of false cause?

In summary, the information screener can be enhanced by providing students with an information-screening strategy that helps them to identify information that seems unreasonable and then to analyze the evidence that has been presented.

THE PROPOSITIONAL NETWORK PROCESSOR

One level of information processing during reading is the propositional level. Many psychologists, such as Walter Kintsch and Teun van Dijk, assert that propositions are the basic units of thought (Kintsch, 1974; Kintsch & van Dijk, 1978; Turner & Greene, 1977; van Dijk, 1977). In simple terms, "a proposition is the smallest unit of information that can stand as a separate assertion; that is, the smallest unit about which it makes sense to make the judgment of true or false" (Anderson, 1990, p. 123). Psychologists Herbert Clark and Eve Clark (1977) noted that there is a finite set of types of propositions. The following sentences represent the major types of propositions:

1. Max walks.

2. Max is handsome.

3. Max eats fruit.

4. Max is in London.

5. Max gave a toy to Molly.

6. Max walks slowly.

7. Max hit Bill with a pillow.

8. Sorrow overcame Max.

Each of these sentences can be affirmed or denied, yet none of their component parts can. That is, you could determine if it is true that "Max walks" or "Max is handsome," but you could not confirm or deny "Max," "walks," or "handsome" in isolation. Proposition, then, might be described as the basic unit of thought.

More complex thoughts are constructed by combining propositions into propositional networks. For example, Figure 4 represents the propositional network underlying the statements "Bill went to the store where he met his sister. They bought their father a coat." As you read, you organize the information into networks like that in Figure 4. The more text you read, the more networks you create.

Central to the process of constructing propositional networks is making inferences. There are two basic types of inferences the reader makes: default inferences and reasoned inferences. Default inferences are those you commonly make about people, places, things, events, and abstractions (de Beaugrande, 1980; Kintsch, 1979; van Dijk, 1980). For example, when you read the sentence "Bill had a dog," you immediately add information such as "The dog had four legs," "The dog liked to eat bones," "The dog liked to be petted," and so on. In other words, you have information stored about dogs. In the

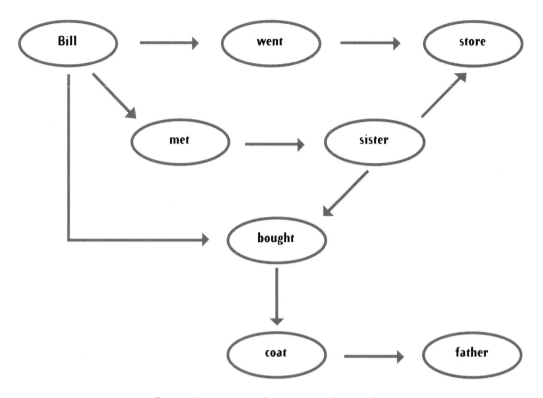

Figure 4: *Depiction of propositional network*

From "Towards a theory-based review of research on vocabulary" (p. 31) by R.J. Marzano n C.J. Gordon. G.D. Labercane, and W.R. McEachern (Eds.) Elementary reading process and practice (2nd ed.). 1993. Needham Heights, MA: Ginn. Copyright 1993 by Ginn. Reprinted with permission.

absence of information to the contrary, you infer that this general information you have is true about the dog, even though it is not explicitly mentioned in the text.

Reasoned inferences are another way that we add information that is not explicit. Such inferences are not part of our general knowledge. Rather, they are "reasoned conclusions." For example, when you read the statement "Experimental psychologists believe that you have to test generalizations to see if they are true" and then later on read about a psychologist who is presented with a new theory by a colleague, you will quite naturally conclude that the psychologist will probably suggest that the theory be tested. This inference comes not from your general knowledge base about psychologists but is induced from the earlier information you read about experimental psychologists.

Default inferences and reasoned inferences, then, help you construct propositional networks for the information in a text. Another way in which you construct propositional networks is through imagery (Kosslyn, 1980). Specifically, researchers in cognitive science have shown that, as you read, you naturally form mental images of the information. Some of these images are literal representations of what you are reading. This commonly occurs when you are reading descriptions of people, places, or things or when you are reading stories. Other images are more abstract in nature. These include concepts and generalizations commonly found in expository texts. These concrete and abstract images are then translated into propositional networks. Imagery is commonly an intermediate step to the creation of a propositional network.

In summary, the propositional network processor creates networks of ideas by making default and reasoned inferences. Additionally, imagery is commonly an intermediary step in the creation of these idea networks. Read Example 3 about Alicia and see if you can identify the propositional network processor in action.

EXAMPLE 3 The following day, Alicia expressed her interest in turtles to her teacher, who suggested that she go to the library to pursue the answers to her questions. The library contained several updated versions of encyclopedias with detailed information pertinent to her questions.

One of the encyclopedias stated that it was a federal offense to bring turtle shells into the United States; all turtle shells brought in were automatically confiscated at customs. Because the older encyclopedia from her home had mentioned that turtle shells were being imported, Alicia concluded that the law had changed. She began to screen the information she was reading more closely, looking for a date when this law was put into effect. She also searched to see if turtle meat or other turtle products not made from the shell were imported.

She learned that different varieties of turtles had identifying patterns and colors on their shells and that some were more beautiful and valuable than others. She noticed that as she was reading, she could envision different shells in her mind. She concluded though, that regardless of the pattern or color, all types of turtle shells were banned from entry into the United States. Alicia became concerned that perhaps the reason turtle shells were not being allowed as imports was because the value of the shells threatened the turtle's existence. Perhaps they were becoming an endangered species.

| DISCUSSION | In this scenario, Alicia was still highly motivated to achieve her goal. She continually screened the information she was reading, making decisions as to whether the information was useful and reasonable. She made a number of inferences as she gathered information about turtles. One of the more important pieces was a reasoned inference that the laws must have changed since the time the encyclopedia in her home was published.

Mediating the Propositional Network Processor

Evidence that a student is having difficulty at the level of the propositional network processor is fairly straightforward—the student has difficulty describing the interrelations among the ideas within the last few sentences he or she has read. For example, a student has just read a paragraph describing how Christmas trees are harvested and brought to market, but all he can tell you about is the Christmas tree his family had last year. Fortunately, there are a number of strategies that can be used to enhance the student's performance in creating idea networks.

Helping Students Make Inferences

One strategy is to help students make inferences to fill in the holes in the information in a text. You can help students generate useful default inferences by helping them identify key concepts that are not explicitly described in the text. To do this, it is useful to have an understanding of the various types of concepts from which default inferences are made.

At a very broad level, there are four general types of concepts: entity concepts, action concepts, event concepts, and state concepts. We are not suggesting that you present the following information on these concepts to students. However, we are suggesting that you have some familiarity with these four types of concepts and their related characteristics. This knowledge will provide a sound foundation with which to generate questions that will facilitate default inferences.

To illustrate, assume that a student is reading a passage in which the concept of equilibrium is central. However, the passage does not provide much explicit information about equilibrium. If you are aware of the four general types of concepts, you will recognize equilibrium as an action concept. Additionally, if you are familiar with the various characteristics of action concepts, you will note that equilibrium has at least two important characteristics that, if not stated directly in a text, must be inferred for the text to make much sense. One of these characteristics might be summarized in the following manner:

> When two elements reach equilibrium, they have usually undergone a change of state relative to their dimensionality (they have changed shape or size), time or duration (they have shortened or lengthened their time or duration to become equal), or intensity (they have lessened or strengthened to become equal).

Entity Concepts

The following outline the various concepts and their attributes (Marzano & Marzano, 1988). Entity concepts usually are concrete and are expressed as nouns. Important attributes include the following:

◻ the concept usually performs a specific action (an umpire)

◻ a specific action usually is performed on the concept (a punching bag)

- the concept commonly is used as an instrument or tool in a specific action (a baseball bat)

- the concept is made in a specific way (wine)

- the concept is part of something (a wheel)

- the concept has specific parts or can be divided up in specific ways (a country)

- the concept has specific characteristics relative to
    - taste (a cake)
    - feel (silk)
    - smell (a skunk)
    - sound (a flute)
    - color (cloud)
    - number or quantity (ants)
    - location (Denver)
    - dimensionality (a diamond)
    - emotional states (a witch)
    - popularity (rock music)
    - commonality (a diamond)
    - danger (a gun)
    - value (a diamond)
    - freedom or ownership (a slave)

Action Concepts

Action concepts usually take the form of verbs and express action. Important attributes include the following:

- a specific person or thing usually performs the action (march)

- a specific instrument is used in the action (swing)

- something is produced as a result of the action (bake)

- as a result of the action, someone or something changes its state relative to
    - smell (fumigate)
    - taste (sweeten)

- feel (wrinkle)
- sound (tune)
- color (paint)
- number or quantity (multiply)
- direction (turn)
- location (send)
- dimensionality (lengthen)
- time or duration (stop)
- freedom or ownership (capture)
- emotional state (frighten)
- popularity (dislike)
- commonness (endanger)
- certainty (threaten)
- value (devalue)
- intensity (negate)

❑ there is a specific process or sequence of events involved in the action (bake); the concept involves
- moving a specific body part (kick)
- grasping an object (hold)
- taking one object into another object (eat)
- expelling an object (cry)
- transferring information (speak)
- acquiring information (listen)
- focusing a sense organ toward a stimulus (look)

Event Concepts

Event concepts are usually expressed as nouns, but they represent actions involving specific times, places, participants, and activities. Important attributes include the following:

❑ the event has specific participants who are normally involved (a wedding)

❑ the event involves a specific process (a football game)

❑ the event has a specific reason or causes specific results (a parade)

❑ the event occurs at a specific time (lunch)

□ the event has a specific duration (dinner)

□ the event occurs in specific locations (a dance)

State Concepts

State concepts usually are expressed as adjectives or adverbs. Their basic function is to describe object, action, or event concepts. Important attributes include the following:

□ there are degrees of possessing the concept (angry)

□ the state conveyed by the concept is acquired in a specific way (tired)

□ the state conveyed by the concept excludes other states from existing simultaneously (dead)

To return to the example, the characteristics of equilibrium could also be discussed as follows: There is a specific process involved in reaching a state of equilibrium (the element greater than the other element on some dimension is lessened in that dimension, or the element lesser than the other element becomes greater in that dimension).

Armed with this awareness, you could then ask the student questions that might help him or her infer key features of the concept equilibrium that are not explicit in the text. For example, you might ask the student questions such as the following:

□ What are some basic changes that occur when something reaches a state of equilibrium?

□ What is the basic process involved in reaching a state of equilibrium?

□ How does this implied information about equilibrium help you understand what you have just read?

A second type of inference is reasoned inference. Although there are many types of reasoned inferences, the ones that are most frequently used by readers deal with premises that "quantify" attributes. For example, when you read that "most sharks are harmless to humans unless provoked" and then later read that a young girl was swimming in an area frequented by sharks, you could reason that the girl would probably not be harmed. To help students make such inferences, you can simply look for statements in the text that quantify attributes. Such statements commonly include quantifiers such as *all, some, many, more, no, few, seldom,* and *never* (Johnson-Laird, 1983). Such statements often set up logical inferences later on in the text.

Once you have identified such statements, you can help students think through reasoned inferences. For example, after identifying the quantitative statement about sharks and the subsequent statement about the young girl swimming, you might help stimulate reasoned inference with questions like the following:

❑ What have you read that will help you draw conclusions about the young girl swimming?

❑ What are the specific implications of the information?

Helping Students See How Ideas Are Linked

In addition to making inferences, the propositional network processor is concerned with linking ideas together in networks or patterns of ideas. Students can be greatly aided in this process by being helped to see common network patterns (Marzano, 1992). What follows are six examples of common network patterns.

Descriptive Patterns
These patterns organize facts or characteristics about specific people, places, things, or events. The facts or characteristics need be in no particular order. For example, information in a film about the Eiffel Tower—when it was built, its height, how many rooms it has—might

be organized as a simple descriptive pattern. This pattern can be represented graphically in the following way:

Sequence Patterns

These patterns organize events in a specific chronological order. For example, a chapter in a book relating the events that occurred during the Cuban missile crisis might be organized as a sequence pattern. This pattern can be represented graphically in the following way:

Process/Cause Patterns

These patterns organize information into a causal network leading to a specific outcome or into a sequence of steps leading to a specific product. For example, information about the events leading to the war in Vietnam might be organized as a process/cause pattern. This pattern can be represented graphically in the following way:

Problem/Solution Patterns

These patterns organize information into an identified problem and its possible solutions. For example, information about various types of grammatical errors that can occur in an essay and the ways of correcting these errors might be organized as a problem/solution pattern. This pattern can be represented graphically in the following way:

Generalization Patterns

These patterns organize information into a generalization with supporting examples. For example, the statement "Important historical events frequently are influenced by chance happenings" is a generalization. We can provide examples for it. This pattern can be represented graphically in the following way:

Concept Patterns

These patterns are perhaps the most general of all patterns. Like descriptive patterns, they deal with people, places, things, or events—but not *specific* people, places, things, or events. Rather, they represent an entire class or category, and they usually illustrate specific examples and defining characteristics of the concept. For instance, information about President Clinton would probably be organized as a simple descriptive pattern—specific facts about a specific president—whereas information about the general concept of presidents might be organized as a concept pattern. The concept of presidents has defining characteristics and specific examples. Concept patterns can be represented graphically in the following way:

Again, we describe how and when you might teach these network patterns to students. However, if students have a basic understanding of these patterns, you can enhance the effectiveness of the propositional network processor by occasionally asking students to organize the information in the last few sentences they have read using one of these patterns. For example, you might say "Create a graphic representation of what you have just read. Try to organize that information using one of the six patterns we have studied or even a combination of those patterns."

Helping Students Identify Images

The final component of the propositional network processor is imagery. As we have seen, a reader continually creates mental pictures. These can be pictures of concrete events and objects or more abstract representations. If the text being read contains information that is fairly concrete, then you might simply ask the student to describe what he or she sees, smells, tastes, touches, or hears. For example, as the student is reading a story, you might occasionally stop him or her and ask questions such as

◻ What mental pictures did the last few lines you read stimulate in your mind?

◻ Was there anything to smell, taste, touch, or hear?

If the text being read contains information that is more abstract, then the image the student creates must necessarily contain symbols. Symbolizing abstract content can be challenging. In fact, a reader must be quite creative in many instances to construct an image for abstract content. Psychologist John Hayes (1981) demonstrated symbolizing abstract content using the following equation:

$$\frac{F = (M^1, M^2) \, G}{r^2}$$

The equation states that force (F) is equal to the product of the masses of two objects (M^1 and M^2) times a constant G divided by the square of the distance between them (r^2). To symbolize this, Hayes recommended the image of two large globes in space, with the learner in the middle trying to hold them apart:

If either of the globes were very heavy, we would expect that it would be harder to hold them apart, than if both were light. Since force increases as either of the masses (Ms) increases, the masses must be in the numerator. As we push the globes further apart, the force of attraction between them will decrease as the force of attraction between two magnets decreases as we pull them apart. Since force decreases as distance increases, r must be in the denominator (p. 126).

Helping students create an image such as this takes time and energy. Quite obviously, that time and energy should be spent only on information that is important to the understanding of the text. However, if abstract information is important to the text, then it is imperative to spend that time and energy. In such cases, the student, with your help, can generate alternate ways of imagining the information until an effective image is produced. For example, regarding the abstract information in Hayes's example, you might interact with a student in the following way: "Let's pull the information in the formula apart. The M^1 and M^2 represent the product of two masses. How could we represent that? How about two globes ..."

In summary, the propositional network processor can be mediated to help students (a) make default and reasoned inferences, (b) organize sets of ideas into networks, and (c) create mental images of concrete and abstract information.

THE WORD PROCESSOR

Perhaps the processing component of reading that has been studied the most is the word processor. Before describing the role of the word processor, it is important to recognize that the words within a proposition are representations of abstractions. That is, when you read, you do not store propositional networks with words in them as depicted in Figure 4. Rather, the components of the idea networks you store in your mind are "concepts." For example, when you represent the proposition (idea) "fish swim" in your mind, the words *fish* and *swim* are not actually stored as components of the proposition. You use words only when you want to express the content of a proposition to yourself or to someone else. Psychologists Turner and Greene (1977) explained

> The actual word or words which are chosen to represent the concept are word tokens for the abstract concept. It

is important to understand that the abstract concept can and may be represented by a number of words in a given language. (p. 3)

In short, the job of the word processor is to recognize words as tokens for concepts. Understanding the job of the word processor, then, is facilitated by an understanding of the nature of concepts. There has been a great deal of research and theory on the nature of concepts. (For example, see the work of Klausmeier, 1980; E. Smith & Medin, 1981.) Virtually all of the research and theory on concepts acknowledges the role of semantic features. Ironically, to exemplify semantic features as they relate to concepts, we must use words that, of course, are not the concepts themselves but only *tokens* for the concepts. With this in mind, consider Figure 5, which illustrates the role of semantic features in defining concepts.

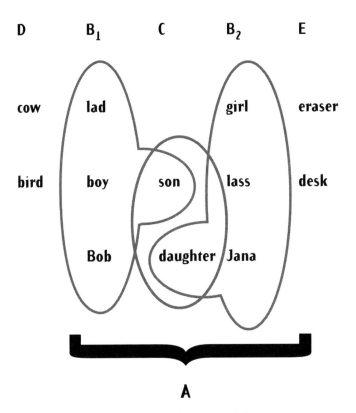

Figure 5: *The role of semantic features in defining concepts*

Semantic feature theory, then, asserts that concepts are defined by sets of semantic characteristics. The concept represented by the word *cow* is defined by semantic features such as animate, concrete, four-legged, milk-producing, and so on. The concept represented by the word *desk* is defined by semantic features such as inanimate, concrete, four-legged, used for paperwork, and so on. Actual words are symbols of or tokens for concepts you have stored in your long-term memory.

One of the most striking features of skillful readers is the ease and speed with which they are able to recognize these symbols or tokens. Skillful readers can course through text at rates of upward of 300 words per minute—upward of 5 words per second. Indeed, Marilyn Adams (1992) explained that skillful readers can perceive whole words as quickly and accurately as single letters. Although the process of recognizing words is probably best described as a set of related subprocesses, one of the primary methods is through spelling patterns. Adams illustrated how we use spelling patterns to understand the following words:

hypermetropical
hackmatack
thigmotaxis

She explained that

> If the above words are new to you, then you could only have read them one way: by decoding them. Yet, for skillful readers of English, decoding such words is easy—so easy in fact, that if you had known the meanings of these words and if they had appeared in meaningful connected text, you might have sped right through them without even noticing whether you had ever seen them before. (p. 54)

In contrast to the ease with which one can decode the previous words, Adams offered the following:

Karivaradharajan
Bydgoszcz
Shihkiachwag
Verkhneudinsk

Adams posed the question, Why are these words much more difficult to read? She provided the following answer:

> The answer, of course, relates to their spelling patterns. These words are not English. Their spelling patterns are unfamiliar. You, as a skillful reader, are very good at decoding, but you do not read from single letters to sounds. Instead you have learned to recognize whole spelling patterns at once ... fluent word recognition does not proceed letter by letter; the fluent reader eventually comes to recognize frequent words and spelling patterns at a glance. (p. 54)

The word processor, then, uses spelling patterns to identify words that are the tokens or symbols for concepts you have learned. But what happens if you do not know the word in the text? Most theorists now believe that you make an initial determination of whether the word is important to the overall meaning of the text. If your determination is that the word is not important, then you skip it. However, if you determine that the unknown word is important, then you try to determine the meaning of the word. You might reread the sentence in which it appeared, looking for clues to its meaning. You might even stop to look up the word in a glossary or a dictionary.

In summary, the word processor facilitates the recognition of words that are tokens for concepts. This is done primarily through common spelling patterns. If the decoded word is not known, the word processor makes a determination of its importance to the overall meaning of the text. If the word is considered key to the meaning of the text, then the reader attempts to figure out the meaning of the word.

To observe the word processor at work, read Example 4.

EXAMPLE 4 One source of information that was very interesting to Alicia was a newspaper article she found that mentioned a man in Miami, Florida who had been caught selling live turtles and had been imprisoned for his actions. The article stressed that anyone bringing in or purchasing this particular species of turtle would be fined and imprisoned.

Some of the words in the article were difficult to recognize. She had not seen them in print before, but once she recognized them she knew what they meant. Some she did not recognize at all. In several cases, she could skip the unknown words and the information in the article still made sense to her. There seemed to be only two words that she could not understand that seemed important to the article. Without knowing these words, the sentences they were in made no sense at all, and this confusion stopped her from understanding the rest of the article. Determined to understand the article, Alicia went to the dictionary to look up the unknown words. One of the definitions made sense to her; however, the other did not, so she took the article and the dictionary to the librarian, Mr. Semaka, for help. He explained the word to Alicia, helping her to get a sense of its use in the article.

DISCUSSION Evidence of the word processor at work is that Alicia could recognize when the words that she did not know were important enough to get in the way of her learning. When this occurred, she had strategies for figuring out what the unknown words meant. One strategy was to consult the dictionary; the other was to ask for help from the librarian, Mr. Semaka.

Mediating the Word Processor

It is usually fairly obvious when a student is not effectively processing words. The basic evidence is that the student has difficulty recognizing the words in the text. He or she skips words, mispronounces words, or replaces words. If the student skips too many words, comprehension breaks down quickly.

Given that the primary way we recognize words is through spelling patterns, a useful mediation strategy is to help a student break an unrecognized word into parts that represent syllables, figure out the sounds of the parts, and then blend the parts together. For example, assume that you were working with Alicia as she was reading the article about turtles. As she read, she came across the word *endanger*. She had heard it before and knew what it meant but did not recognize it in print. You would help her divide the word into syllables: *en/dan/ger*. You would then ask Alicia if she recognized any of the "parts"—in effect, if she recognized any spelling patterns. Alicia might recognize the patterns in the syllables *dan* and *ger*. You could then help her blend these recognized spelling patterns together. Certainly Alicia would have to make a number of attempts at sounding out the word. However, with some coaching, she would eventually recognize the word in print as the one she knew when it was spoken.

Another mediation technique is to provide students with an explicit strategy for dealing with words they cannot recognize. What follows is a four-step strategy:

1. Skip the word and read to the end of the sentence.

2. Go back to the word and ask, "What word would make sense here and begins with this letter or letters?"

3. If unable to determine the unknown word, reread the previous sentence or continue reading the next sentence and try Steps 1 and 2 again.

4. If still unable to recognize the word, identify a word that would make sense and continue reading.

The techniques described here are effective mediation devices if a student is simply having difficulty decoding the orthographic representation for words for which he or she has internalized concepts. However, students may have difficulty recognizing words because they have not developed the concepts that the words represent. The best way to determine if this is the case is to simply ask students about the words they miss. That is, when a student misses a word, you would simply state the word for the student and ask if he or she understands it. For example, assume the student skipped or mispronounced the word *equilibrium*. You would say, "That word is equilibrium. Tell me what it means." If the student indicates that he or she knows the word, it probably means that the student is simply having trouble decoding the words in the text. He or she knows them but cannot recognize them. Consequently, the four-step strategy described here would be warranted. However, if the student does not know the words, then it is an indication that he or she has an inadequate store of concepts for the text he or she is reading. It may be the case that the text is too difficult for the student given his or her present level of knowledge about the topic. This might simply be alleviated by obtaining a simpler text on the topic.

It might be the case, however, that the student has a relatively small sight vocabulary—those words that the student can recognize by sight. This, of course, is a much more serious issue. In this situation, helping the student is basically a matter of increasing his or her sight vocabulary.

Research by William Nagy and his colleagues (Nagy, 1988; Nagy & Anderson, 1984; Nagy, Anderson, & Herman, 1987; Nagy, Herman, & Anderson, 1985) indicated that wide reading is one of the best ways of increasing one's vocabulary. Specifically, Nagy estimated that if students spend 20 minutes per day reading at a rate of 200 words per minute for 200 days of the year, they would read a million words annually (Nagy & Herman, 1987). Given this amount of reading, children would encounter 15,000 to 30,000 unfamiliar words and would learn between 750 and 1,500 of them.

> A period of sustained silent reading could lead to substantial yearly gains in vocabulary, probably much larger than could be achieved by spending the same amount of time on instruction specifically devoted to vocabulary. (Nagy & Herman, 1987, p. 26)

In summary, the word-processing component of reading can be enhanced by providing students with specific decoding strategies. In a more generic sense, word processing is enhanced by developing a student's base of concepts through extended wide reading.

THE MACROSTRUCTURE GENERATOR

The ultimate product of the reading process is a macrostructure. Psychologists such as Kintsch and van Dijk explained that a macrostructure contains the "gist" of what is read. Figure 1 represents this as occurring after the other processes. In fact, the creation of a macrostructure occurs throughout the reading process. That is, as you read something, you construct your own representation of the basic gist of that information. That representation is formed by the use of what van Dijk and Kintsch referred to as *macrorules*. Specifically, van Dijk and Kintsch (1983) identified three basic macrorules that can be described in the following way:

1. Deletion—Given a sequence of propositions, delete any proposition that is not directly related to the other propositions in the sequence.

2. Generalization—Replace any proposition by one that includes the information in a more general form.

3. Construction—Replace any set of propositions by one or more that include the information in the set stated in more general terms.

According to these rules, when you create a macro-structure, you construct a parsimonious representation of the information that does not include specific details about what you read but includes the general outline of the information. This explains why you usually do not remember the specific facts in an interesting story that you read but do tend to recall the general flow of information and events (e.g., "There was this boy and girl from different sides of the town. One was very rich and one was very poor. The rich one met the poor one ...").

Example 5 about Alicia depicts the results of the macrostructure generator.

EXAMPLE 5 Having explained the unknown word to Alicia, Mr. Semaka asked her about the information she had gleaned from her reading. She explained that there were many animal coverings that were prohibited as imports into the United States because the value of their coverings could cause them to become endangered. She explained that sometimes a law may permit certain animal coverings to be imported, but when people begin to see that it is endangering the very existence of the species, people fight to change the law. She also explained that although you cannot bring animal coverings into the United States, it may be okay to bring in other parts of the animals. Mr. Semaka asked her for an example of what she meant and she explained that in the newspaper article she learned that you could not bring in live turtles but that some restaurants serve turtle soup, so it must be okay to import turtle meat. Mr. Semaka then asked her if she thought that requests for turtle soup would also contribute to turtles becoming an endangered species. Alicia concluded that this was a good question and decided to pursue the answer for herself.

DISCUSSION Alicia's explanation to Mr. Semaka provided a snapshot of the information in her macrostructure about turtles. Notice that she did not present a detailed description of what she had read; rather, she presented a broad description of the relation between laws and endangerment. She had internalized the basic gist of the information she had gathered. Her initial question that led her to pursue the information in the first place had, to some degree, been answered. Her conversation with Mr. Semaka spurred her on to continue in her exploration of turtles.

Mediating the Macrostructure Generator

Again, it is fairly clear when the student is not processing information effectively at the macrostructure level. The student might be able to provide specific pieces of information about the text but cannot articulate the overall structure and intent of the text. For example, the student might be able to provide you with specific names, facts, and events about a story or even specific episodes but be unable to articulate the general flow of action and the plot.

One of the best ways of helping the student enhance macrostructure processing is to provide him or her with summarizing and paraphrasing strategies. Research by Ann Brown and her colleagues (A. Brown, Campione, & Day, 1981) indicates that the following set of steps is one of the most powerful summarization strategies:

1. Delete trivial material that is unnecessary to understanding.

2. Delete redundant material.

3. Substitute superordinate terms for lists (e.g., flowers for daisies, tulips, and roses).

4. Select a topic sentence, or invent one if it is missing.

To help a student in this process, wait until he or she has completed reading the text or a major section of the text. The, guide him or her through this strategy by asking questions such as

❑ Which information was unnecessary to understanding the text?

❑ Which information was central to understanding the text?

❑ Was there any information that was redundant—that was simply a repeat of what was said before?

❑ What are some terms or ideas that capture the important information we have identified? Can you think of a sentence or two that puts all these ideas together?

The macrostructure processor, then, can be enhanced by the use of a specific strategy.

SUMMARY

For each of the five components of the reading process, there are specific behaviors that indicate difficulties in that particular component. In addition, there are specific techniques and strategies that can be used to facilitate each type of processor. In this section, we have briefly outlined some of those techniques and strategies. Consider the information you have just read and answer the following questions.

1 Which reading processing component seems the most complex to you and why?

2 What are some of the possible implications you now see for mediating the reading process?

3 If you recently assigned an informational reading passage, such as in a science or social studies text, what strategies did you use to help students set a purpose for reading? What additional mediating strategies might you wish to try now?

4 As you recall typical reading assignments used in your classrooms, which ones fully engaged students as critical readers? Which future assignments might you give to students that will allow them to apply the information in this section on logical fallacies?

ANSWERS TO QUESTIONS

We hope that your answers to Questions 1 and 2 include some of the following:

1 There is no one right answer here, but many people perceive the propositional network processor as the most complex because it involves generating inferences, creating patterns, and constructing images.

2 Possible implications include:

- ◻ more time must be spent one-on-one with students
- ◻ a thorough knowledge of the reading process on the part of the teacher
- ◻ a good rapport between teacher and student
- ◻ the teacher acting as facilitator

goal three

Understanding and Mediating
the Writing Process

Just as the reading processing components operate in a parallel or simultaneous fashion, so too do the processing components of writing. These are depicted in Figure 6.

An alternate representation of the interaction of these processing components is presented in Figure 7.

Again, it is important to recognize that this is a very simplified model of writing. For our purposes, however, it is useful for illustrating the process of guiding students during mediated instruction. Much more complex models have been depicted by Linda Flower and John Hayes (Flower & Hayes, 1980a, 1980b, 1981a, 1981b; Hayes & Flower, 1980), Robert de Beaugrande (1980), and George Hillocks (1986, 1987). We consider each processing component in some depth, along with ways of increasing students' skills and abilities in the various processing components.

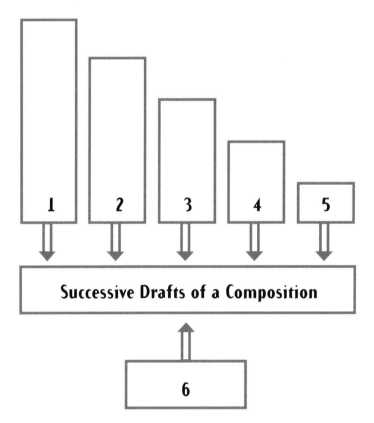

1. The general task processor
2. The network processor
3. The sentence processor
4. The word processor
5. The graphemic processor
6. The editorial processor

Figure 6: *Process components of writing*

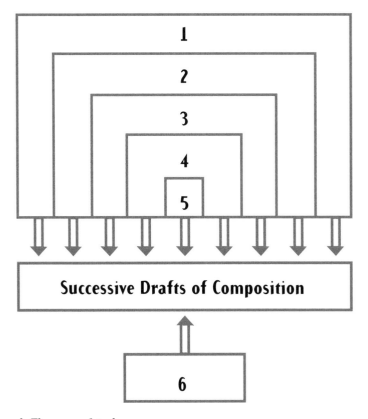

1. The general task processor
2. The network processor
3. The sentence processor
4. The word processor
5. The graphemic processor
6. The editorial processor

Figure 7: *Alternate model of writing process components*

THE GENERAL TASK PROCESSOR

In writing, the general task processor deals with three basic elements: (a) the purpose of the writing, (b) the audience for whom the writing is intended, and (c) the adequacy of the information. Just as the process of reading is driven by goals or purposes, so too is the process of writing. However, a unique feature of the composition process is that your purpose for writing affects the format or type of discourse you use. For example, if your purpose is to persuade, then you will probably write in what has been termed *argumentative discourse*. If your purpose is to express emotion, then you might select poetry as the form of discourse. Traditionally, the following types of discourse have been taught to students, although theorist James Britton (1970, 1978) has proposed other labels:

narration
description
exposition
argumentation
poetry

In 1980, psychologist Teun van Dijk (1980) proposed further categories such as editorials, research papers, descriptive essays, stories, and so on.

Regardless of the classification system followed, it is important that the writer can translate his or her purpose into a fairly specific structure. That is, when you decide that you wish to create a vicarious experience for the reader, you must be familiar with a structure like a story or a poem to carry out your purpose.

Audience is another basic concern of the general task processor. Consideration of audience has a direct effect on what you select to include in and exclude from in a composition. Specifically, psychologists Herbert Clark and Eve Clark (1977) showed that when writing (and speaking), people follow the general principle of not including a great deal of information that is already known by the audience. The "old" information included is usually just a reference point for or a foundation on which to build the "new" information presented. This is called the *given/new contract*. Quite obviously, if you write for an audience who is knowledgeable about a topic, your writing will be quite different from that written for an audience who is not knowledgeable about the topic.

Finally, the general task processor deals with the adequacy of the composer's knowledge base. That is, the effective writer continually asks, "Do I have to gather more information to complete this?" If the answer is yes, the writer stops composing and gathers the needed information.

The general task processor, then, monitors three basic aspects of the composing process: (a) the purpose of the writing, (b) the audience for whom the composition is intended, and (c) the information base that is being used to construct the composition.

For a description of the general task processor at work, read Example 1 about Troy.

> **EXAMPLE 1** In eighth-grade English class, Troy had been reading Romeo and Juliet. It seemed to him that Romeo and Juliet faced situations similar to those that teenagers face today, such as violence and social pressure. In fact, over the past few months his community had been plagued by drive-by shootings by teenagers who were seeking membership into gangs.
>
> Troy had been very annoyed by the local newspaper articles that stated that teenagers today were not as responsible as the teenagers from previous generations. The guest editorial columns bothered him the most. The writers of these editorials usually made broad claims about today's teenagers but offered little evidence to back up their claims.
>
> Troy decided that he would write his own editorial and submit it to his local paper for publication. An editorial would allow him to state his position and cite support for his claims. Because he though his audience members could range from 18 to 80 years in age, Troy concluded that he should probably remind his older readers of their own teenage years and the irresponsible actions of some of their peers. Because most people do not know about or have forgotten the irresponsible actions of teenagers of past generations, he concluded that he would have to provide his readers with a great deal of specific information.

DISCUSSION In this scenario, Troy's goal to make a claim and support it with evidence led him to consider the editorial format. His conclusion that his audience probably knew or remembered little of the evidence supporting his claim meant that he would be writing for an audience that knew little about his topic.

Mediating the General Task Processor

Evidence that a student is experiencing difficulty with the general task processor includes the following:

❑ The writing has no clear purpose. You cannot determine whether the student's composition is intended to relate a story, present information, or present an argument.

❑ The writing has no clear audience. The writer makes frequent references to things the audience is not aware of and/or goes into detail regarding material with which the audience is familiar.

❑ The writer does not have an adequate information base. The writing is very general and lacks specific detail.

One basic mediational technique to improve general task processing is simply to help students clarify their purpose, identify their audience, and examine the adequacy of their information base. For example, to help a student clarify his or her purpose, you might ask the following:

❑ What are you trying to accomplish in this composition?

❑ Are you trying to tell us a story?

❑ Are you trying to describe something?

□ Are you trying to explain something?

□ Are you trying to help us experience a specific emotion?

Because the writer's purpose is related to the type of discourse he or she will use, it is important that the student identify the specific type of discourse that will best reflect his or her purpose. Recall that there are a number of ways to classify types of discourse. For mediational purposes, it is useful to think of generic discourse structures—large organizational patterns that circumscribe an entire book or an entire essay. Troy used an editorial organizational pattern for his composition. These patterns are commonly referred to as superstructures. Here, we consider three basic *superstructures*: (a) the narrative, (b) the T-R-I structure, and (c) the argumentation structure.

The narrative superstructure has six basic components:

Setting	The main character is introduced along with information about the time, place, and context in which the story occurs.
Initiating event	An event sets the story in motion, causing the main character to respond in some manner.
Internal response	The characters display internal reaction to the initialing event. This reaction results in some goal or goals.
Attempt	The characters engage in a series of actions carried out to attain a goal.
Consequence	An event or events mark the attainment or nonattainment of the goal.
Reactions	The characters in some way express their reaction to the consequence.

If a student identifies the narrative superstructure as the one that best fits his or her purpose, you might guide him or her to a consideration of the various components of this discourse structure by asking questions such as

❑ Who will be the characters in your story?

❑ Where will your story take place?

❑ When will your story take place?

❑ What will start the action rolling in your story?

The T-R-I superstructure is commonly used when one's purpose is to present information supporting a generalization. T-R-I stands for *topic*, *restriction*, and *illustration*. The topic is a very general statement about the information to be discussed. The restriction limits the information in some way. The illustration exemplifies the restrictions. The following series of sentences show how these elements combine to form a T-R-I superstructure:

Topic	The 1981 Braves were the best team in baseball.
Restriction	Their pitching staff was excellent.
Illustration	Bill Johnson was 20–2 for the season.
Illustration	Bob Ewy had the fastest pitch in the majors.
Restriction	Their hitters were also excellent.
Illustration	Dave Walton batted .421.
Illustration	Walter Zebleman hit 42 homers.

If a student has identified the T-R-I superstructure as the one that will best serve his or her purpose, you might help him or her articulate the various elements of a T-R-I pattern by asking questions such as

❑ What is the topic or the most general statement in the information?

◻ How is the topic limited or restricted?

◻ What are the examples or illustrations of the restrictions?

Another common discourse superstructure is the argumentation superstructure. It has four basic components: observation, claim, elaboration, and qualifier. The following examples show how these components work together to form a argumentation superstructure:

Observation   Information that leads to a claim. For example, "Last night, five crimes were committed within two blocks of one another."

Claim   A general assertion that something is true. For example, "The crime rate in our city is escalating dramatically."

Elaboration   Examples of or explanations for the claim. For example, "The dramatic increase can be seen by examining the crime rates in the downtown area over the last twenty years. For example, in 1970 …"

Qualifier   A restriction on the claim or on the evidence supporting the claim. For example, "The crime rate has stabilized in some areas of the city, however …"

If a student has identified the argumentation superstructure as the one that best serves his or her purpose, you might help him or her identify the specifics of this structure by asking questions such as

◻ What is your base claim?

◻ What observations did you make that lead to the claim?

◻ What is your evidence for the claim?

◻ What restrictions do you want to put on your claim?

These three superstructures—narration, T-R-I, and argumentation—are only a few of the many that students might use. For a more exhaustive listing of useful superstructures, including those such as the editorial superstructure used by Troy, see the works of Frank d'Angelo (1980) and Teun van Dijk (1980).

Another way to mediate the general task processor is to help students clarify the audience for whom they are writing. The basic issue regarding audience is to establish how much the audience knows about the topic. That is, because good writers have a clear-cut perspective regarding the knowledge base of their audience, they know what they do and do not have to explain to their audience. To help a student clarify this issue, you might tell the student to pretend that you are the audience for which he or she is writing and ask questions like the following:

❑ If I were your audience, what would you have to explain to me if you thought I didn't know the information?

❑ What wouldn't you have to explain because you assume I already know it?

❑ Who do you want to read your composition?

❑ What will you have to explain to them in detail?

❑ What do they already know about your topic?

Finally, the general task processor deals with the sufficiency of the writer's information base. In effect, the efficient writer is constantly monitoring whether he or she needs to gather more information for the composition. You can help students identify the extent to which they need to gather more information about the topic by asking, "What do you intend to say in your composition?" If they have difficulty supplying specifics about what they are going to present, then you might suggest possible sources for more information.

In summary, the general task processor can be mediated by helping students identify a purpose for writing and the most appropriate discourse structure for that purpose by helping students clarify what their audience does and does not know and by helping students determine the adequacy of their information base.

THE NETWORK PROCESSOR

Within the reading process, the reader translates the words and sentences into networks of ideas called *propositional networks*. Within the writing process, the writer begins with basic ideas that might be likened to propositional networks. That is, the writer begins with abstract skeletons of ideas. Part of the task of writing is to fill out this skeleton. Carl Bereiter and his colleagues (Bereiter, Fine & Gartshore, 1979; Bereiter & Scardamalia, 1982, 1985) referred to these abstract skeletons of ideas as "gist units"; George Hillocks (1987) described a gist unit as "a generally circumscribed unit of content that has not been laid out in any detail, but for which the writer probably has notions of form and purpose" (p. 73). In nontechnical terms, Bereiter and Hillocks said that before you actually put words on paper, you have an idea of what you wish to write (or say).

To illustrate, when writing a letter to a friend, you probably think in "chunks" of ideas. At a certain point in the letter, you know you want to describe your new car. You are not exactly sure what specific aspects of your car you will detail, but you do know that the next set of sentences will be descriptive in nature. In the next part of your letter, you will explain a particular incident that happened to you in your new car. Again, you are not sure what you will say, but you know that you want to relate this particular episode. These two chunks of information—the description of your car and the account of the episode in your car—are the gist units described by Bereiter and Hillocks, the abstract skeleton of ideas.

Read Example 2 about Troy for a depiction of the network processor.

EXAMPLE 2 As Troy rehearsed what he might like to include in his editorial, he thought in terms of networks of ideas. He thought he might begin by describing an incident in which a group of teenagers were doing something considered antisocial. Next, he would describe the reactions of adults to this incident. He would quote the adults as saying that teenagers were becoming more irresponsible each year. Next, he would explain that the incident and the quotation about it came from the Roman empire about 100 B.C. This would be a good beginning section of his editorial. Troy then began to think about the body of his editorial.

DISCUSSION Notice how Troy tended to think in large chunks of ideas—first he would describe an incident, then explain what adults might say about it, and so on. These large networks of ideas were placeholders for the specific sentences Troy would compose.

Mediating the Network Processor

When students are having difficulty processing information at the network level, their sentences do not seem to hold together as logical "sets." That is, individual sentences and even pairs of sentences may make sense in isolation, but strings of three, six, ten, and even more do not hold together well. Rather, the writer produces sentences that seem disconnected to the whole.

To help students think in terms of sets of ideas, it is useful to encourage them to think in terms of patterns or networks of thought. Fortunately, the same basic patterns can be used in writing that are used in reading. Recall that we described six basic patterns when we described the reading process:

1. descriptive

2. sequence

3. process/cause

4. problem/solution

5. generalization

6. concept

To mediate the network processing component of writing, you can ask students questions that help them identify the patterns they might use to express their thoughts. These questions include

☐ Is there something you want to describe here?

☐ Is there a sequence of events you want to relate?

☐ Is there a process you want to describe?

☐ Is there a problem with its possible solution you want to identify?

☐ Is there a generalization for which you will provide examples? Is there a concept you want to describe?

To illustrate, assume that you were working with Troy as he wrote his editorial. If you noticed a set of sentences that did not seem to hold together as a group, you might conclude that Troy's network processor was not functioning well as he composed that particular section of the editorial. You would ask Troy questions like those just listed. These questions should help Troy identify the basic pattern of thought he wished to convey. ("Well, I really wanted to describe some possible solutions to the problem of gang violence in this section.")

In short, mediating the network processing component of writing is a matter of helping students think in terms of sets of ideas.

THE SENTENCE PROCESSOR

When you actually begin to put words down on paper, the sentence processor begins to operate. Hillocks (1987) explained the nature and function of this processor in the following way:

> Writers appear to have a general notion of what is to be written (semantic units) and proceed to work out the specific lexical items to produce what Bereiter calls a verbatim unit, a sequence of words not yet recorded, but which the writer can state on request. (p. 73)

Just as in the reading process, the basic unit of thought in writing is the proposition. Constructing a sentence involves combining a number of propositions. As Clark and Clark (1977) stated, "At the core of the sentence to be planned are propositions—units of meaning that reflect the ideas speakers want to express" (p. 237). In short, a sentence usually contains a number of propositions. To illustrate, consider the following sentence:

> Bill bought the red sedan that had been sitting in the store window for two weeks.

This sentence is a product of the following propositions:

> Bill bought the sedan. The sedan was red. The sedan had been sitting in the store window for two weeks.

To construct the original sentence, the writer combined these independent ideas (propositions) into a single sentence. This process of combining propositions occurs in a predictable fashion. Anne Matsuhashi's (1981) research indicates that when planning a sentence, the writer usually thinks in terms of clauses beginning at the front end of a sentence. That is, when you compose a sentence, you work out what you will say in the first clause starting with the subject, continuing to the verb, and so on. Then you consider the next clause in your sentence and so on. Hillocks (1987) described this process in the following way:

> The semantic units appear to include keys to the kind of structure to be produced, though not the specific lexical items. That is, while the semantic unit may necessitate that a certain kind of relationship be established (e.g., temporal, cause/effect), it allows for choice among a variety of specific syntactic and lexical structures. At this level, a writer may review alternative constructions and choose one in light of its appropriateness to purposes, content, and form. (p. 73)

As Hillocks' (1987) remarks imply, constructing a sentence does not always progress smoothly. Sometimes the structure of the first clause makes it difficult or even impossible to express the ideas (propositions) intended for the second clause in a way that is grammatically correct. It is the job of the sentence processor to coordinate the combining of groups of propositions into sentences that are grammatically correct and convey the message intended by the writer.

Read Example 3 to observe the sentence processor in action.

EXAMPLE 3 After thinking about the overall structure of his editorial, Troy was ready to put his thoughts on paper. Some sentences seemed to flow right from his mind to the paper. More often than not, though, he began a sentence but then got stuck in his thinking. He knew what he wanted to say, but he could not figure out how to say it given the way he had started the sentence. He began one sentence with "Adults have forgotten their dissatisfaction with life when they were young ..." He also wanted to say that this blinds them from seeing the reasons why young people act out against society, but he could not think how he could say it without making the sentence long and cumbersome. He finally decided to start the sentence a different way: "Adults of today can't understand why teenagers have a need to break the rules because adults have forgotten the dreams they had when they were young about the way life could be." Then the next sentence seemed to flow easily: "This is one of the main reasons for the generation gap ...," but the next sentence produced another set of problems.

DISCUSSION The sentence processor was clearly at work in Troy's composing. He was trying to put ideas (propositions) together in sentences, but he had to follow the rules of standard English as he did so. Sometimes he got himself into syntactic binds—the way he began a sentence did not allow him to add the remaining ideas to the sentence without breaking some grammatical rule or constructing a clumsy sentence. In this case, it was best to "back up" and start over.

Mediating the Sentence Processor

When students are having difficulty at the sentence-processor level, their sentences are commonly ill-formed—the first half of the sentence might not sound like it goes with the second half or the student constructs a pair of sentences that have no apparent relationship or have an incorrectly marked relationship.

To aid students in sentence-level processing, it is useful to make them aware of the basic relationships that propositions can have within and between sentences. There are four general types of relationships that propositions can have with one another:

Addition

One proposition adds equivalent information to another, or one proposition is stated as similar to another. For example,

Bill is tall and handsome. Bill, who is tall
and handsome, ….

Contrast

One proposition is identified as contradictory to another
or does not go well with the other. For example,

He is tall but not very good at basketball.

Cause

One proposition is the cause or condition of another.
For example,

He went home because she went home.

Time

One proposition is identified as occurring before, during, or after another. For example,

She left before he did.

Each of these four basic types of relationships have
the following subtypes:

Addition Subtypes

Modification	The **tall** boy plays basketball.
Equality	He is tall **and** he is handsome.
Restatement	I am tired. **In fact**, I am exhausted.
Example	She does many things well. **For example**, she is excellent at cards.
Summation	He does many things well. He cooks. He sews. **In all**, he is an excellent homemaker.

Contrast Subtypes

Antithesis	I will be there, **but** I won't be happy.
Alternative	**Either** it will rain **or** it will snow.
Comparison	Bill is tall. In **comparison**, his brother is short.

Concession	I don't like violence. **Nonetheless**, I'll meet you at the fights.

Cause Subtypes

Direct cause	He won the race **by** maintaining his concentration.
Result	Bill went home. **Consequently**, the party ended.
Reason	He went to the store **because** he needed food.
Inference	Mary is going on a long trip. **In that case**, she should plan well.
Condition	**Unless** you stop, I will leave.

Time Subtypes

Subsequent action	They went to the game. **Afterward**, they went to the dance.
Prior action	They went to the dance **after** they went to the game.
Concurrent action	Bill thought about Mary **while** Mary thought about Bill.

Each of these types of relationships also uses specific words or phrases to signal the relationship. The signal words in the sentences just listed are in bold type. The various signal words that can be used for each type of relationship are listed in Exhibit 1 (Haggerty, Valencia, & DiStefano, 1987, p. 176).

Again, we show in the next section how you can provide students with direct instruction in these relationship markers. However, you can stimulate an awareness of these relationships while engaged in mediation by asking students to clarify the relationships they have stated in their sentences. For example, assume that a student has incorrectly indicated an additive relationship between two clauses by using the connective *and*. You might help the student clarify the type of relationship he

Time

Afterward, next since, then, after that, in the end, shortly, subsequently, so far, as yet, before, until, finally

After, earlier, initially, in the beginning, originally, at first, previously, beforehand, formerly, before that, before now, until then, up to now, by now, by then

Simultaneously, while, meanwhile, meantime, at this point, at the same time

Cause

By, consequently, hence, now, so therefore, thus, as a consequence, for all that, as a result, whereupon, accordingly, the result was, this is the reason why

Because, because of, in that, so that, since, so on account of, for the fact that

Else, otherwise, in that case, then

Now that, providing that, supposing that, considering that, granted that, admitting that, assuming that, presuming that, seeing that, unless … then, as long as, in so far as, if, where … there, when … then, no sooner …

Addition

Which, that, who, whom, when, where, and, moreover, equally, too, besides, furthermore, what is more, likewise, similarly, as well, in addition, besides, at the same time

Indeed, actually, in actual fact, in fact, namely, that is to say, another way of saying this

For example, first, second, third, one, two, three, …, for a start, to begin with, next, then, finally, last but not least, for one thing, for another thing, another example would be

Altogether, over all, then, thus, in all, therefore, all in all, in conclusion, in sum, in a word, in brief, briefly, in short, to sum up, to summarize

Contrast

But, yet, or rather, what is better, what is worse, contrariwise, conversely, oppositely, on the contrary, else, otherwise, on the other hand

Alternatively, either … or, neither … nor, rather than, sooner than

In comparison, in contrast, like

However, anyhow, besides, else, nevertheless, nonetheless, only, still, though, in any case, in any event, for all that, in spite of that, all the same, anyway, though, at any rate, regardless of this

From *Reading diagnosis and instruction: Theory into practice* (p. 176) by R.J. Marzano. P.J. Haggerty. S.W. Valencia. and P.P. DiStefano. 1987. Englewood Cliffs, NJ: Prentice-Hall. Copyright 1987 by Prentice-Hall. Adapted with permission.

or she intended by asking questions such as "You are indicating that these two ideas go together or are alike in some way. Are you sure that is the type of relationship those two ideas have? Is there another type of relationship between the two ideas you would like to indicate?"

According to research, clarification of relationships among propositions will help alleviate one of the major problems students have in writing. Specifically, Shaughnessy (1977) illustrated that students frequently use words and phrases that signal specific types of relationships in situations in which the relationships do not in fact exist. For example, a student might use the signal word *but* to connect two propositions that do not in fact have a contrasting relationship. In short, mediating the sentence processor involves making students aware of the need to clarify the relationship between the propositions in the sentence and the sets of sentences they compose.

THE WORD PROCESSOR

The word processor is responsible for selecting the exact words that are used in the construction of a sentence. The words selected might best be considered an initial selection of words from the reader's lexicon of words. Metaphorically, we might say that each writer has a list of words he or she can use to represent the concepts in the propositions he or she produces. This list of words is sometimes referred to as the writer's *lexicon*. Your lexicon contains the words for the concepts you understand.

As you produce a sentence, you search through your lexicon to identify the word you want to use to express a concept within a particular proposition. Skilled writers have many words from which they can select to represent a given concept. They have many options and can consequently come up with specific selections quickly and efficiently. Unskilled writers have few words from which to select. Fewer options render the selection process highly inefficient and constrained. Sometimes unskilled writers do not even have a word in their lexicon that truly expresses the concept they want to convey. In this case, the composing process breaks down. The writer cannot express his or her thoughts.

In summary, the word processor is concerned with selecting words that represent the concepts within the propositions that the writer is constructing. These words are selected from a mental listing or lexicon of words that are the tokens for the concepts the writer knows. For a depiction of the word processor at work, read Example 4 about Troy.

> **EXAMPLE 4** | As Troy was putting his ideas down on paper, he selected the words that would best express his thoughts. Occasionally, he had to stop and think about the word he wanted to use. He wanted to say something about the impact of the frustration of teenagers, but he was not familiar with the word *impact*. He thought of different ways to express this idea. He considered a few possibilities:
>
> > result
> > effect
> > product
>
> He finally settled on the word *effect*.

> **DISCUSSION** | Troy's thinking as he searched for words to express his thoughts illustrates that we sometimes have a concept in mind but do not have a word that expresses the exact meaning of that concept. The more words in your lexicon, the more effective you are at expressing your thoughts.

Mediating the Word Processor

Evidence that a student is not effectively processing at the word level includes use of the same word over and over again. To illustrate, consider the following:

> The fire began small. Then it became a big fire. It was such a big fire that many people had to come to fight the fire. Some of the people lost their lives in the fire.

These sentences seem quite immature. One of the main reasons is that the student has overused the same words. *Fire* is used five times; *people* and *big* are each used twice. Now consider the difference in the sentences when a variety of words are used to express the same concepts:

> The fire began small. Then it developed into a huge blaze. It grew so large that a number of people had to come to fight it. Some of the fire fighters lost their lives in the catastrophe.

One way to help students at the word-processor level is to point out the overuse of specific words. For example, if you were interacting with the student who wrote the first group of sentences, you would point out the overuse of the words *fire, people,* and *big*.

Another indication that a student is having difficulty at the word-processing level is lack of precision in word choice. To illustrate, consider the following:

> He was kind of a philanthropist.

> Even in her hour of mourning, she was not let alone by the curious onlookers.

> With regards to the time limit you have given me, I must now ask for an extension.

Each of these sentences contains an example of imprecise use of words. In the first sentence, the use of the words *kind of* is a precision error. Technically, the words *somewhat of* should have been used. In the second sentence, the word *let* is inappropriate. The verb *let* should not be used for the verb *leave*. In the third sentence, *regards* is used imprecisely. The appropriate phrase to use in this sentence would be *with regard to*.

Precision of word choice presumes a knowledge of how words should be used. Unfortunately, this must occur at the individual word level. That is, each word has fine nuances of meaning. The rules that govern the use of one word might have little or no relationship to the rules that govern the use of other words. We learn these subtle rules and fine distinctions of meaning by experience with the language. For example, it is experience that teaches us when we should use the word *infer* instead of the word *imply* and the word *accept* instead of the word *except*. Pointing out students' imprecise use of words will have a cumulative effect. Over time, they will learn the nuances of the words they use.

In summary, mediating the word processor is a matter of making students aware of the overuse or the imprecise use of certain words.

THE GRAPHEMIC PROCESSOR

As you select words to represent the concepts in the sentences you compose, you naturally attempt to spell those words correctly. Of course, you already know the spelling of many of the words you select. These words are reproduced directly from memory. Those words for which you do not know the spelling present a problem, however. You either make an attempt to spell them correctly and go on, or you stop to ensure that the spelling is correct.

An interesting feature of the graphemic processor is that it can get in the way of the smooth execution of the other processes if too much attention is paid to it. That is, if you stop too long to figure out how to spell a word, it will inhibit your thinking within the other processing components. For example, if you stop the composing process too long to figure out how to spell *pneumonia*, you may lose track of your thinking about the sentence you are trying to construct or the network of ideas you are trying to translate into sentences.

In summary, the graphemic processor deals with the correct orthographic representation or spelling of words. When you cannot spell a word from memory, you might stop to figure it out. However, too long a pause might inhibit the other processing components. Read Example 5 to see how a student might use a graphemic processor.

EXAMPLE 5 Troy selected the word *effect* to express a specific concept in a particular sentence. As he wrote the word, he thought to himself, "Is it e-f-f-e-c-t or is it a-f-f-e-c-t?" He settled on "a-f-f-e-c-t." Most of the words he wrote he could spell quite easily—right from memory. However, once in a while he selected a word that he was not sure how to spell. Sometimes he had alternative spellings in mind, such as with *affect* and *effect*. Other times he had no clear idea about how to spell the word. In these cases, he guessed about the spelling of the word on the basis of how it sounded.

DISCUSSION Troy's experience is fairly typical of a young writer—he could recall the spelling of some words but often encountered words that he did not know how to spell. In such cases, the graphemic processor became the focal point of his attention in that all his energies were devoted to constructing an acceptable spelling for the word.

Mediating the Graphemic Processor

Evidence that a student is processing ineffectively at the graphemic level is an overabundance of misspelled words in the first draft of a composition. It is important to note that almost all first drafts include misspelled words. Here, however, we are referring to an overabundance of misspelled words.

On the positive side, many times students need only be shown that they have misspelled a number of words and they correct their mistakes. For example, as students are writing, you might simply point out their misspellings and they will correct them. In this case, the student probably was not paying attention to spelling while writing, and your cuing helped refocus his or her thinking. On the other hand, many students do not have a sufficient store of words that they can spell correctly. In this case, they will have to make a concerted effort to build up a store of words that they can spell with little conscious thought.

It is important to note that overemphasizing errors in the word processor or graphemic processor can negatively affect a student's writing ability. That is, if students are worried about selecting the perfect word or about spelling every word correctly while composing, they will have little space available in their working memory to concentrate on the higher levels of processing such as network and sentence processing. Additionally, within the writing process, problems that occur at the network, sentence, word, and graphemic processing levels can be cleared up in the editing phase of writing.

THE EDITORIAL PROCESSOR

The final aspect of the composing process is the editorial processor. In this model, the majority of activity one would consider editing occurs after the completion of an initial draft of the composition, although it is certainly the case that some editing can occur simultaneously with the other processes. During editing, the writer is most concerned with making sure that the information is presented in a logical flow and that the mechanics of the English language have been adhered to.

It is important to note that the term *revision* has not been used in this model. Revising generally means making major changes in the basic structure and/or intent of the discourse. Hillock (1987) described revision as "re-examination of a whole discourse, or some fairly extensive part of it, after the first version of that discourse has been completed. Revision in this sense involves the re-examination of the whole product in light of purposes, content, and form" (pp. 73–74).

There is evidence indicating that writers occasionally make significant changes in their compositions. For example, Flower and Hayes (1981b) described a young man changing the form and content of his essay after reconsidering his audience. However, what writers and teachers commonly refer to as revision is more local in nature and is probably best described as extended editing. For example, as reported by Hillocks (1987), high school seniors averaged 61 revisions per piece of writing. The vast majority of these were cosmetic and mechanical and are best described as editorial considerations. No students changed basic purposes, content, or form. Hillock explained that this is not as drastic as the figure suggested:

> We should not be shocked by these findings. How many of us, after producing a first draft, scrap the entire manuscript? We may do it occasionally, but not often. What provokes larger scale revisions has not been studied in any detail ... (p. 74)

Again, consider in Example 6 Troy's writing.

EXAMPLE 6 Troy had set his editorial aside for a few days and had then come back to it. Reading it over, he saw whole sections that needed to be rewritten. He also identified some sections that needed to be added. He made these changes and then set the editorial down again. When he came back to it in a few hours, he read it over again. This time he noticed some sentences that were clumsy. He rewrote these. He also noticed some grammar errors and tried to correct these. After making a few other changes, he concluded that the editorial was ready to be sent to the newspaper. However, right before he mailed it to the newspaper, he read it again and found a few more changes he wanted to make. Even though it took him an extra hour to make these last-minute changes, he did so because he wanted the editorial to be perfect.

DISCUSSION Troy's example illustrates that the editorial processor is usually activated repeatedly. That is, effective writers edit in layers or cycles. During one cycle, the writer might look for certain types of changes; during another cycle, the writer attends to other types of changes.

Mediating the Editorial Processor

The fact that the editorial processor is activated after the writer has produced workable drafts of his or her composition makes the writing process significantly different from the reading process given that we do not usually engage in "drafts" of reading a particular text.

During editorial processing, the writer can go back and clear up any problems that occurred within the other processors. Evidence that a student is having difficulty with the editorial processor is that the final draft of his or her essay has many errors.

There are many different elements that should be considered during editing. Many of these are described in Shaughnessy's *Errors and Expectations* (1977). Here, we consider the following types of errors:

1. omissions, insertions, and substitutions

2. mixed patterns

3. dangling and misplaced modifiers

4. overreduction

5. lack of parallelism

Omissions, Insertions, and Substitutions

Consider the following sentences:

> I feel that my extending her stay she made the situation worse.

> Life is really hard today, so you can imagine what it will in the future.

> I felt that like he was my friend.

All of these sentences contain specific types of errors. The first sentence contains a substitution error:

The word *my* is substituted for *by*. Usually a substitution error looks very much like the word it is substituted for. The second sentence contains an omission error: The word *be* has been omitted from the sentence. Omission errors occur frequently, especially in first-draft writing. The third sentence contains an insertion error: The word *like* should not be there. If it were left out, the sentence would be logical and correct. What usually happens when insertions errors are made is that the writer's mind is considering two or three ways of expressing a thought. When the sentence is recorded, parts of both structures are written.

Errors of omission, insertion, and substitution are almost impossible to avoid. All writers produce them, and the best safeguard against them is a careful reading aloud of an essay. Usually omissions, substitutions, and insertions will jump out at a student during this oral proofreading. Other types of errors are not as obvious, however.

Mixed Patterns

Consider the following sentence:

> Statistics show that the average person's future a college education will greatly enhance his earning power.

In this sentence, the phrase *the average person's future* does not make sense. The writer might have had the following two possibilities in mind:

> Statistics show that an average person's future earning power will be greatly enhanced by a college education.

> Statistics show that on the average a college education will greatly enhance a person's earning power.

The author incorporated elements of both structures in the sentence, producing a mixed pattern. Mixed-pattern errors are similar to insertion errors, except that the former involve larger chunks of the alternative patterns. Mixed-pattern errors can thus be more difficult to correct than insertion errors. Sometimes a writer must pull the sentence apart to identify what he or she actually intended to say. This is best done by trying to phrase the sentence in different ways until finding a pattern that makes sense. The following are examples of mixed-pattern errors and alternative structures that are phrased using correct grammatical structures:

Mixed pattern

> If a person feels that by joining the armed forces could improve his future he should probably look into the Navy.

Alternative structures

> If a person feels that joining the armed forces could improve his future, he should probably look into the Navy.

> If a person feels that by joining the armed forces he could improve his future, he should probably look into the Navy.

Mixed pattern

> To take keypunching you must go to a computer school for it.

Alternative structures

> To take keypunching you must go to a computer school.

> You must go to a computer school for keypunching.

Dangling and Misplaced Modifiers

What is wrong with the following sentence?

> Getting into the car, the engine wouldn't start.

It is not clear what the phrase *getting into the car* modifies. There is nothing in the main clause that it could modify: The only noun in the clause is *engine* and certainly the engine was not getting into the car. Such a construction is called a *dangling modifier*, which is a modifying clause, phrase, or word that does not clearly modify anything. A general rule regarding modifiers is that they should be placed as close to the word or words they modify as possible. For example, consider the following sentence:

> Having been told he was using unacceptable procedures, the judge held the lawyer in contempt of court.

The phrase *having been told he was using unacceptable procedures* is meant to modify *lawyer*, but it is placed in such a way that it looks like it modifies *judge*. Consequently, it is considered a misplaced modifier. We can correct the error by moving the modifying phrase as close to the word it modifies as possible—preferably right before or after it. The sentence should read as follows:

> Having told the lawyer that he was using unacceptable procedures, the judge held him in contempt of court.

Overreduction

Sometimes students are guilty of overreduction or overconsolidation of ideas, which results in the grouping of too many ideas into a sentence. To illustrate, consider the following sentence:

> The boy next door, who has been living there for the last ten years which have been very pleasant considering the tone of the times, realized that this peaceful, quiet town is just not exciting enough for an individual like himself, who would like to succeed as much as possible in life and affect as many other lives as possible.

There is nothing technically wrong with this sentence. It violates no stated rules of grammar. There are so many ideas packed into it, however, that it is difficult to understand. Probably the information stated in the sentence would be better expressed as two or three sentences:

> The boy next door recently came to a realization. He had been living in that house for the past ten years—very pleasant years considering the tone of the times. He realized that this peaceful, quiet town was just not exciting enough for an individual like himself, one who would like to succeed as much as possible in life and affect as many other lives as possible.

These sentences are far less confusing than the original sentence. This is not to say that long sentences are always incomprehensible: Effective writers frequently use very long sentences, but they do so in such a way as to express their ideas clearly and unambiguously. The basic issue is whether there are so many ideas expressed in a sentence that the reader gets lost. If so, those ideas should be expressed in two or more shorter sentences.

Lack of Parallelism

Parallelism means using similar structures to express similar ideas. Consolidating ideas can create the syntactic problem of lack of parallelism. This frequently occurs when verbs from two sentences are consolidated into one statement with a compound predicate. For example, consider the following sentences:

> I agree that a father should share his son's experiences. I also think that it is a father's responsibility to help his son when in need.

Logically, these two sentences can be consolidated and reduced because they repeat similar concepts—that a father has certain responsibilities and duties to a son.

When combining these sentences one might produce the following:

> I agree that a father should share his son's experiences and to help his son when in need.

The problem with this sentence is the lack of parallelism of the structures used to express the two verbs (*share* and *to help*). One is expressed as a main verb with a modal (*should share*) and the other as an infinitive. The sentence should read as follows:

> I agree that a father should share his son's experiences and help his son when in need.

A general rule of thumb when consolidating or combining ideas is that parallel ideas should be expressed in the same syntactic structures.

In addition to the types of errors just described, there are some other common ones that are usually cleared up during editing. These include

▢ Lack of subject–verb agreement

▢ Lack of agreement between pronoun and antecedent

▢ Improper use of verb tense

▢ Improper punctuation

▢ Improper capitalization

We do not discuss these here because there are many excellent reference texts that discuss them in depth, such as Millword and Bowie's *Workbook for Writers* (1980).

The mediational technique for all of these is the same. Have students read their composition orally or read it aloud to them. Students can usually hear that something is wrong with each of the types of errors mentioned here.

In general, it is very difficult to edit simultaneously for all of the components discussed in this section. Many times writers edit first for those aspects of writing in which they know they are weak. You can help students greatly in the editorial process by pointing out or helping them discover weak and strong points. For example, if you have noticed that a student has a preponderance of poor word choices and overused words, you might suggest that he or she concentrate on the word process aspect of writing in the initial editing.

SUMMARY

The writing process involves six processing components that operate in a parallel fashion. Problems with each processing component can be identified by looking for specific types of evidence. Additionally, each processing component can be enhanced during mediation by providing students with information and strategies specific to each processing component. Before moving on to the next chapter, reflect on the following questions.

SELF-DIRECTED QUESTIONS

1 Which components of the writing process do you think are the hardest to bring to the conscious level of students and why?

2 Which component of the writing process do you think is the most complex and why?

3 Which future assignments might you give that will allow students to write for different purposes or for different audiences?

4 In which writing process component are your students weakest? How do you plan to address these weaknesses?

ANSWERS TO QUESTIONS

We hope that some of your answers to Questions 1 and 2 include the following:

1 There is no one right answer to this question. However, many people select the network processing component and the sentence processing component. These are difficult to bring to the conscious level because they are so automatic. They deal with the expressions of propositions and sets of propositions. If, in fact, the mind naturally thinks in proposition form, then it would be difficult to be aware of such thinking.

2 Again, there is no single answer to the question. However, many people select the editorial processor because it deals with the components of all the other processors. When we edit, we have to reconsider all the other processors.

goal four

Mediated Instruction

in the Classroom

In this section we discuss practical ways of structuring class time to accommodate the approaches we have outlined. The types of mediational activities described in the two preceding sections clearly require one-to-one interaction between teacher and student. One way of approaching mediated instruction is to schedule time for this interaction, particularly with students who are experiencing difficulties. As costly in terms of time, energy, and resources as this is, it appears worth the effort, as evidenced by Clay's (1979, 1981) success with teaching beginning reading. As we mentioned, this text is an attempt to do for upper elementary, middle school, junior high, and high school what Clay did for the primary grades with her process for mediated instruction. Her approach requires a significant amount of one-to-one interaction with students, singling out for extensive mediation those students who are experiencing difficulty learning to read. The success of such intense focus is well documented.

We assert that there is little doubt that the reading and writing performance of students, even those experiencing severe difficulties, can be greatly enhanced by focused mediated instruction. We also recognize that this requires the commitment of a great many resources—a commitment that many schools and districts are probably not in a position to make at this time. In the interim, there are ways in which mediated instruction can be integrated into traditional classroom practices. However, to do so, the traditional classroom must be radically restructured. Fortunately, an instructional format does exist that facilitates the necessary restructuring. It is referred to as the *workshop approach*.

The workshop approach, popularized by Nancy Atwell (1987), Lucy Calkins (1986), and Jane Hansen (1987), has three components: (a) a mini-lesson, (b) an activity period, and (c) a sharing period. These are depicted in Figure 8.

We consider each of these components in some detail.

THE MINI-LESSON

A mini-lesson is just that—a brief lesson. It is a time devoted to direct instruction. It can last from 2 to 15 minutes. The mini-lesson is the time when specific information and strategies that can be used to mediate the reading and writing processes are taught to the whole class. If you re-read the sections of this book that pertain to Goals 3 and 4, you will find that specific elements of both processes lend themselves to direct instruction. For example, within the reading process, the following aspects might be directly taught to students in a mini-lesson:

1. The general task: the three general purposes for reading and their implications

2. The information screener: an information-screening strategy; the three categories of errors commonly made in the presentation of evidence

3. The propositional network processor: various types of local patterns; concrete and abstract imagery techniques

4. The word processor: spelling patterns; a strategy for mediated word recognition

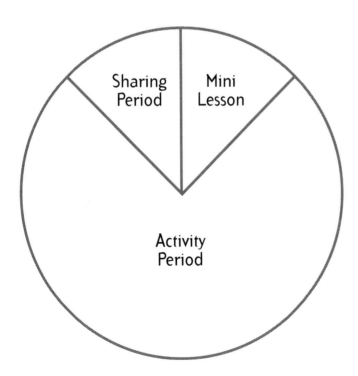

Figure 8: *Lesson divided into workshop component parts*

5. The macrostructure generator: summarizing and paraphrasing strategies

Similarly, the following aspects of the writing process lend themselves to direct instructions within a mini-lesson:

1. The general task processor: various discourse superstructures

2. The network processor: local patterns of thought

3. The sentence processor: types of relationships between propositions; signal words for relationships

4. The word processor: usage rules regarding specific words and phrases

5. The graphemic processor: spelling patterns

6. The editorial processor: specific types of errors that are commonly corrected during editing

The decision of what to teach in a mini-lesson is made on the basis of student needs. If you notice that a number of students are having difficulty using a certain type of discourse superstructure within the general task processing component of writing, then you would present a mini-lesson on that particular type of superstructure. For example, assume that you observed many of your students having difficulty writing compositions that support a generalization when their purpose is to provide information. You might conclude that it would be useful to expose students to the T-R-I superstructure. During the mini-lesson of a particular workshop, you would present this discourse superstructure to students, providing clear examples of topics, restrictions, and illustrations using content with which students are familiar and interested. For example, you might find an example of a T-R-I pattern in a sports magazine article or in a newspaper editorial. As a whole class, you would discuss the nature of topics, restrictions, and illustrations using the two examples. As a class, you might also generate a few outlines of possible T-R-I patterns using topics about which students are currently writing. The mini-lesson is a time to present information pertinent to the reading and writing processes to the entire class. One useful planning technique is to create a classroom profile of student strengths and weaknesses relative to components of the reading and writing processes. Figure 9 contains a blank profile that might be used to document students' strengths and weaknesses.

Class: *4th Period*

Reading	Writing
Class Strengths:	Class Strengths:
Class Weaknesses:	Class Weaknesses:

Figure 9: *Classroom profile sheet*

THE ACTIVITY PERIOD

The activity period is the core of the workshop approach. It lasts much longer than the mini-lesson, commonly 40–60 minutes or longer. The following two activities take place during this time: (a) the teacher works with individual students on a one-to-one basis and (b) those students not working with the teacher work independently in pairs or in small groups on projects.

Working One-to-One With Students

During the activity period, you meet with individual students in a "mediational conference" format. That is, you work with individual students to provide mediation in reading, writing, or both. If you and the student are working on reading during the conference, the student should bring something to read. Ideally, the material the student selects should be highly interesting to the student and a little challenging. It is very important to note that the student should select the reading material.

When working with the student, begin by making him or her feel at ease. Emphasize that this is not a test—the two of you are simply going to work on skill development. The student then begins to read orally. During the student's oral reading, it is your job to look for possible problems in the various processing components of reading. That is, attempt to determine if the student is having difficulty with the general task processing component of reading or with the propositional network processing component, and so on. This will take a keen eye on your part. To aid in your analysis, it is useful to have the student occasionally stop reading and describe his or her thinking. This description should provide some insights into the various processing components. To obtain the most robust information, it is useful to occasionally ask the student to respond to questions such as the following:

◻ Can you describe what you have read in the last few sentences?

◻ How does this relate to your overall purpose for reading?

◻ How does this relate to the rest of the information you have read?

◻ Is there anything you've read that does not seem reasonable? Why?

◻ What information do you have to add to the text so that it makes sense?

◻ Which words have been hard to understand?

As the student reads and describes his or her thinking, look for evidence of strengths and weaknesses in the various processing components of reading. Below, we review the types of evidence indicating problems in the various processing components.

1. The general task processor: The student's attention frequently wanders.

2. The information screener: The student does not or cannot respond to direct questions regarding the reasonableness of the information.

3. The propositional network processor: The student has difficulty describing the interrelations among the information in the last few sentences read.

4. The word processor: The student has difficulty recognizing fairly simple words.

5. The macrostructure generator: The student cannot summarize or paraphrase the overall gist of the information.

For example, while the student reads, you might note that his or her attention wanders. This would be an indication that he or she does not have a clear purpose for reading or has forgotten that purpose (i.e., difficulty with the general task processor). You might then help the student clarify his or her purpose. Additionally, you might notice that the student cannot describe the relationship among the ideas in the last few sentences. This could indicate that he or she is having difficulty with the propositional network processing component of the reading process. You could then help the student organize small chunks of information using various patterns.

In short, during a mediational reading conference, you use your knowledge of the reading process to help students improve their reading skills while they are involved in the act of reading. To keep track of your interaction with students during mediational reading conferences it is useful to keep a log of your interactions with each student. Figure 10 contains a sample log.

If you are working with the student on the writing process, ask the student to bring a composition that is not quite complete. It is important that the student selects a composition on which he or she is currently working to ensure a high degree of interest on the student's part. Ask the student to continue writing in your presence. Again, you might occasionally ask the student to stop and respond to questions such as

❏ What were you trying to convey in the last few sentences you wrote?

❏ How does this relate to your purpose for writing your composition?

❏ What is their relationship to the previous sentences?

❏ Why did you select that specific word?

If the student has already completed a first draft of the composition, ask him or her to edit it in your presence. Analyze the student's editing for indications that

Student: *Jeanne Deak*

Date	Observations	Actions
10/8	Jeanne's attention seems to wander while she reads. I don't think she establishes clear goals before reading. She doesn't do well at describing the relationships among the ideas in the last few sentences she has read. This is a network processing problem.	I helped her set a goal for her reading and this seemed to help. I'm going to try teaching her some patterns to see if this improves her network processing.

Figure 10: *Sample log entry*

he or she is aware of and correcting the various types of errors that are controlled for by the editorial processor.

Again, look for the specific types of evidence during the student's writing and editing. The following is a review of the types of problems indicating difficulty with an area of the writing process:

1. The general task processor: The writing has no clear purpose; the writing has no clear audience; the writing lacks specificity.

2. The network processor: Sentences do not hold together in logical sets.

3. The sentence processor: Individual sentences and pairs of sentences are ill-formed.

4. The word processor: Words are overused; words are used imprecisely.

5. The graphemic processor: There is an abundance of spelling errors in the first draft.

6. The editorial processor: The final draft of the composition has many errors.

If you see evidence indicating a difficulty with any component of the writing process, bring it to the student's attention and attempt to mediate that processing component. For example, if you noticed that certain sentences and pairs of sentences were ill-formed, this would be an indication that the student was having difficulty at the sentence-processing level. You might mediate this processing component by helping the student clarify the relationships between propositions. Additionally, if you noticed that a student was continually using the same word to express a single concept, this would be an indication that he or she was having difficulty with the word-processing component. You might then mediate this component by helping the student identify alternate words and phrases to express the concept. Again, it is useful to record your interactions with students in a log like that in Figure 10.

In summary, during the activity period you work with individual students on a one-to-one basis. This one-to-one interaction provides the opportunity for you to mediate the processes of reading and writing. But what are the other students doing while you are working with individual students?

Projects

While you are working one-to-one with an individual student, the remainder of the class is working on projects. The concept of a project is certainly not new. In fact, it dates back to the early work of John Dewey and William Kilpatrick (Pulliam, 1987). Basically, a project is a task that mirrors the complexity and holistic nature of real-world tasks. Specifically, projects are tasks that are (a) partially specified, (b) multidimensional, (c) student-directed, and (d) long-term.

Partially Specified

Specification refers to the extent to which the final product of a task is predetermined. There are some tasks for which the outcomes are totally determined or fully specified. Consider, for example, answering questions of the multiple choice, true/false, fill-in-the-blank, matching, or short-answer variety. The outcomes of these tasks are fully specified in terms of structure and content; hence, while engaged in them students have little, if any, chance of creating new knowledge. A partially specified task, on the other hand, provides students with the flexibility to design the format and content of the final product.

Multidimensional

Closely related to the characteristic of partial specification is multidimensionality. Multidimensional refers to the variety of mental operations that are used within a task and the variety of ways that the task can be completed. Although such tasks are not easy to construct, there are some useful models. In some of our own work (Marzano, 1992), we have found the following seven tasks to be very complex in that they involve a variety of mental operations but are useful at virtually every grade level and in every content area:

Task	General purpose
Decision making	Making an informed selection among equally appearing alternatives.
Historical investigation	Developing an explanation for some past event and then supporting that explanation.
Projective investigation	Developing a scenario for some hypothetical event and then supporting that scenario.
Definitional investigation	Describing the defining characteristics of some concept for which the characteristics are not self-evident.
Problem solving	Developing, testing, and evaluating a method or product for overcoming an obstacle or constraint.
Experimental inquiry	Generating, testing, and evaluating the effectiveness of hypotheses generated to explain a physical or psychological phenomenon and then using those hypotheses to predict future events.
Invention	Developing a unique product or process that fulfills some articulated need.

To illustrate the variety of cognitive operations inherent in these tasks, consider the component parts of each task:

Decision making

❑ identifying the alternatives to be considered

❑ identifying the criteria used to assess the alternatives and their relative importance

❑ identifying the extent to which each alternative possesses each criteria

❑ making a selection of alternatives

Historical investigation

❑ identifying a historical event to study

☐ using as many primary sources as possible, identifying the alternative explanations for the historical event and the discrepancies behind these explanations

☐ selecting one of the alternative explanations or constructing a new explanation

☐ defending the selected or constructed explanation ·

Projective investigation

☐ identifying a hypothetical event to study

☐ identifying the alternative opinions that exist regarding the hypothetical event

☐ selecting one of the alternative opinions or constructing a new one

☐ defending the selected or constructed opinions

Definitional investigation

☐ identifying an ill-defined concept to study

☐ identifying the alternative positions regarding the defining characteristics of the ill-defined concept

☐ selecting a position or constructing a new one

☐ defending the selected or constructed position

Problem solving

☐ identifying the important factors affecting the problem situation along with the characteristics of the desired outcome and the constraints or obstacles in the way of achieving the desired outcome

☐ identifying the standards or criteria for a successful solution

☐ identifying the possible alternative ways of overcoming the obstacle or the constraint

☐ selecting and trying out an alternative

☐ identifying the extent to which the selected alternative produces a solution that meets the stated standards or criteria

◻ if other alternatives were tried, articulating the reasoning behind the order of their selection and the extent to which each meets the stated standards or criteria

Experimental inquiry

◻ explaining a phenomenon initially observed

◻ identifying the facts or principles behind the explanation

◻ making a prediction on the basis of the facts and principles underlying the explanation

◻ setting up and carrying out an activity or experiment to test the prediction

◻ evaluating the results of the activity or experiment in terms of facts and principles that have been articulated

◻ making another prediction of future events on the basis of the combined information from the original explanation and results of the activity

Invention

◻ identifying a situation needing improvement or an unmet need

◻ identifying a purpose for the invention

◻ identifying specific standards or criteria the invention will meet

◻ developing a rough model, sketch, or outline of the product

◻ developing the product

◻ continually revising and polishing the product until it reaches a level of completeness consistent with the criteria or standards that were articulated

As illustrated, each task is cognitively complex and requires a variety of interdependent mental operations. For example, while engaged in decision making, a learner must select an issue about which to make a decision, weigh the importance of various alternatives, and judge the extent to which alternatives possess identified characteristics. Options are available within almost every step of each task. For example, while performing the task of invention, the learner has options as to the situation or need to attend to, the purpose of the invention, and the standards used to judge the invention.

What follows are sample tasks that could be used in the English and language arts classroom.

EXAMPLE | **DECISION MAKING**

You have been asked to suggest which of the various genres should be included in the new school library. Your task is to work with two other people to determine what criteria would be important for selecting the new books, the various genres you might include, and your two top choices based on your decision-making process. You will present your choices to the school librarian in the form of a business letter. Your letter must include the reasons for your decision and should reflect all of the characteristics of a business letter.

EXAMPLE | **HISTORICAL INVESTIGATION**

As you have been reading your science-fiction novel, we have been identifying the characteristics of the genre of science fiction. But how did this particular genre come about?

In groups of four, go to a variety of resources to see if you can discover what is known about the first science-fiction novels ever written and published. Are there any disagreements as to who wrote and/or published the first ones? Present your findings to the class in an oral report. Along with your report, include evidence that you involved another person to peer edit your report.

EXAMPLE | PROJECTIVE INVESTIGATION

You have just finished reading *The Phantom Tollbooth* by Norton Juster. Imagine that you are Milo as he traveled through the lands of Dictionopolis and Digitopolis in his phantom tollbooth. What if there had been another land—a new region to travel called *The Kingdom of Wisdom*? What would that have been like? Consider what your travels might be like in that kingdom, how they would differ from the travels in the other two kingdoms, and how the people might be different from the ones you have already met.

Working with a partner, produce a comic book, news report, television broadcast, or play that depicts what your travels would be like.

EXAMPLE | DEFINITIONAL INVESTIGATION

Each of the books the class has been reading has emphasized friendships that people have and what happens as a result of those friendships. But each friendship seems to be different. What is a friend?

Form a group of three people in which each has read a different book. Examine the friendships that are represented in each of the books to determine what it means to be a good friend. Look for any agreements or contradictions that exist among the books.

Using this information, create a definition for the word *friend*. Present this definition to your classmates in the form of a survey. Have students react to your definition and then report the results to your class. If there were people who did not agree with your definition, present a logical explanation as to why they did not agree.

| EXAMPLE | **PROBLEM SOLVING** |

You have just finished reading the story *Sarah Plain and Tall* by Patricia MacLachlan. In this story, Sarah faced many problems on the farm. She faced fire, drought, planting crops, wind, and loneliness.

Imagine what this story might be like if the setting had been New York City in 1993 instead. Sarah has come to New York in response to an advertisement in the *New York Times* to marry a man with two children.

Working with a partner, identify some of the problems Sarah might face. Create a diary Sarah might have kept that shows what some of these problems might be.

| EXAMPLE | **EXPERIMENTAL INQUIRY** |

Certain books in our class library seem worn and tattered, and yet many students seem to select these books to read even though they are not in very good condition. Draw a picture that explains why you think students select these books. Try to include as much detail in your picture as possible. When you have finished your picture, conduct a study about why students read some books and not others. Select four books that seem worn. Next, find three students in your class who have read each of these books. Interview them to find out why they read these books. After gathering all this information, examine the reasons and determine if your original prediction seems to be accurate. Present your finding to the class in the form of a chart, graph, or other graphic representation.

┌─────────────┬──────────────┐
│ **EXAMPLE** │ **INVENTION** │
└─────────────┴──────────────┘

You have just finished reading a survival novel and you have identified the major items necessary for survival specific to the setting of your novel. Form a group with two of your classmates who have also read survival novels. Consider the survival criteria you each selected from the settings in your respective novels. What criteria would be necessary for survival in one book but not in another?

Use this information to examine the plight of the homeless in today's society. Using the telephone, interview the people who are in charge of the homeless shelters in your city. Gather information about the shelters and how they provide for the list of basic needs you have established on your survival list. Using the information from your interviews, develop a plan to improve the homeless shelters in your community. Once you have your plan in place, ask some of your classmates to read it to see if they have any suggestions or concerns. Make any improvements or revisions as necessary and submit your plan, along with a letter of explanation, to your local city councilperson.

Student-Directed

Student-directed refers to the extent to which students construct and direct the execution of a task. Ideally, students are allowed to specify all components of the task. Student-directedness within decision making, for example, means that the student, rather than a teacher, specifies the alternatives to be considered, the criteria to be used to assess the alternatives, the extent to which the alternatives meet the criteria, and the final selection.

Student-directedness also refers to the freedom and opportunity to identify the manner in which the outcomes or final products of the task will be reported. This means that students have choices other than the characteristic written essay or oral report. For example, each of the following methods is a valid way of reporting the results of a project and may allow students to capture the process of their effort as well as the products.

☐ a videotape

☐ a newscast

☐ a graphic organizer with an explanation

☐ a slide show

☐ a dramatic presentation

☐ a demonstration

This list can be expanded even further if students are allowed and encouraged to develop artifacts along with their tasks. Artifacts are physical or artistic products (e.g., a song, a poem, a mural, poetry, sculpture) that represent some aesthetic or symbolic by-product associated with a task. For example, within a decision-making task about which action would have been best for the United States to take against Iraq in the Gulf War, a student might develop a sketch as a supplement to a written report. Whereas the written report communicates the process used in the decision-making task and the conclusions drawn from it, the artifact (the sketch) communicates a specific affect associated with the conclusions drawn in the report.

Long-Term

Quite obviously, the types of tasks described in this section require time—some of them two or even three weeks. Consequently, students must be given time to complete them. They might work on these tasks individually, in pairs, or in small groups. The longevity of these tasks has practical benefits by allowing the teacher time to interact with students on a one-to-one mediational basis. For example, assume that activity periods last an average of 45 minutes. Also assume that each individual mediational conference lasts an average of 10 minutes per student. Consequently, you could meet with 4 students in a single period, 20 students in a week, and so on. Over a quarter or semester period, you could meet with each student several times.

THE SHARING PERIOD

The final component of a workshop is the sharing period. Here students are invited to share any insights or issues that have come up during the workshop. One student might share an insight he or she had as a result of a mediational conference with you. Another student might share a problem he or she has encountered with a project and might ask for suggestions from the group. In short, the sharing period is simply a time when the entire class interacts as a unit—a time to build the culture of a community of learners.

SUMMARY

The workshop format allows teachers to work with students on a one-to-one basis so that they can mediate the various components of the reading and writing processes. Additionally, projects are vehicles that allow students to be involved in tasks that are partially specified, multidimensional, student-directed, and long-term. Both of these activities are powerful learning experiences for students. During mediation, students receive focused help in specific processing components of reading and writing. During projects, students are engaged in robust tasks that mirror real-world situations.

1 What do you think is the basic dynamic of a mediational conference?

2 What do you feel is the basic purpose of projects?

3 Construct a task that is partially specified, multidimensional, student-directed, and long-term (as described in this section) that you might use in your class.

4 Select a student from your class with whose reading or writing you are very familiar. Identify the strengths and weaknesses of that student in reading or writing and the mediational strategies you might use to address his or her weaknesses.

ANSWERS TO QUESTIONS

1 During a mediational conference focused on reading, the student reads a text of his or her own choosing. The teacher looks for evidence of difficulties with various processing components. If a difficulty is identified, the teacher provides information or strategies that can aid the student in the particular processing component. During a mediational conference focused on writing, the student writes a composition or edits in the presence of the teacher. Again, the teacher looks for specific problems and offers specific information and techniques.

2 Projects allow students to work alone or in small groups on tasks that mirror real-world situations. Additionally, they provide time when a teacher can work with individual students in mediational conferences.

Revisiting Mr. Navarro
and Ms. Zimmer

In this book, we describe how the current research and theory on reading and writing can be used to enhance students' skills and abilities through mediational instruction. Our intent is that you use the information in this text to alter your instructional practices to enhance the learning of your students. To see how you might use this information, take a moment to re-read the scenario about Mr. Navarro and Ms. Zimmer on pages 3-4. How would you change both classrooms to make them more compatible with the principles you learned in this book? When you are finished, read our discussion of those two classes.

Mr. Navarro's class exhibits many effective characteristics. Students are doing a great deal of reading over which they have much control. Additionally, they are engaged in a great deal of self-directed writing. However, there is no overt skill development in Mr. Navarro's class. Without intervention by Mr. Navarro, some students (perhaps many) may not develop skills that are vital to reading and writing development. In short, Mr. Navarro should start interacting with students on a one-to-one basis as they read and write, with the intent of enhancing the development of specific skills.

Ms. Zimmer's class emphasizes skill development but does so outside of the context of reading and writing. Her use of worksheets and seatwork to practice reading and writing skills does not necessarily translate into skill development. Ms. Zimmer should integrate her emphasis on skill development with the acts of reading and writing. She, too, needs to interact with students while they are engaged in the reading and writing processes, providing expert guidance and encouraging practice.

To provide such guidance and practice, Mr. Navarro and Ms. Zimmer must be highly knowledgeable about the nature and function of the various reading and writing processing components as well as strategies that can be used to enhance each component.

Final Review

This book has provided a framework for interacting with students in such a way as to enhance their competencies in reading and writing. It draws from two philosophies that were once considered incompatible—the skills approach and the whole-language approach. When considered from their extreme positions, the two approaches can appear diametrically opposed. The skills approach operates from the following assumptions:

☐ The processes of reading and writing are composed of skills that are organized in a hierarchic fashion.

☐ These skills are executed from the most specific to the most general—from the bottom up.

☐ Given the flow of information from the bottom up, the most specific skills of reading and writing should be mastered before the more general ones are attempted.

The whole-language approach, however, operates from very different assumptions:

☐ The reading and writing processes involve the execution of skills or component parts, but the whole is greater than the sum of its parts.

☐ The flow of information within the component parts progresses from the most general components to the most specific—from the top down.

☐ Given the holistic and top–down nature of reading and writing, instruction should focus not on individual skills but on engaging students in robust, authentic reading and writing tasks.

Fortunately, these two perspectives can be combined into an instructional approach that emphasizes the following:

☐ engaging students in holistic, robust reading and writing tasks

☐ intervening with students as they read and write to help them enhance specific processing components of reading and writing

We refer to this approach as *mediated instruction*. To be effective at mediated instruction, a teacher must have a thorough understanding of the reading and writing processes. We have conceptualized reading as involving five processing components:

1. The general task processor, which controls for the general purpose of reading

2. The information screener, which judges the extent to which information appears reasonable

3. The propositional network processor, which organizes ideas from sets of sentences into compact networks of ideas

4. The word processor, which deals with the recognition of words

5. The macrostructure generator, which constructs a parsimonious representation of the information in the text

We have conceptualized writing as involving six processing components:

1. The general task processor, which controls for the general purpose for writing, the intended audience, and the adequacy of the writer's information base

2. The network processor, which constructs specific patterns of thought that will be translated into sentences

3. The sentence processor, which translates idea networks into coherent sentences

4. The word processor, which selects words to represent concepts

5. The graphemic processor, which analyzes spelling patterns to recognize words

6. The editorial processor, which deals with correcting errors after a first draft has been constructed

For each processing component, a teacher seeks to recognize student strengths and weaknesses and provide assistance when weaknesses are identified.

Finally, to use mediated instruction in the classroom, a teacher must reorganize the traditional class period. We have suggested that a class period be divided into three segments:

1. The mini-lesson, which is a brief instructional period during which the teacher presents students with strategies that might be used within the reading or writing processes and with information that they might use while doing projects.

2. The activity period, which is an extended period of time during which students work on long-term projects that involve reading and writing. While students are working on projects, the teacher meets with individual students. During these conference sessions, the teacher provides mediated instruction in reading and writing.

3. The sharing period, which is a brief period during which students are encouraged to share their insights and experiences.

This book has attempted to provide a solid start in developing the knowledge base a teacher needs to be effective at mediated instruction. However, we emphasize that what we have provided is only a beginning. To use what cognitive psychology has disclosed about reading and writing, you must be a student of those processes. In other words, to be an effective teacher of literacy, you must be an effective student of the research and theory on literacy. This book, as well as others in this series, was designed to be a useful resource for serious students in that endeavor.

Glossary

Basal reader—A series of reading books and supporting workbooks that traditionally teach and reinforce skills in a specific order. Many modern basal readers have more of a whole-language orientation.

Concept—An abstract entity defined by its semantic features and represented by various words.

Editorial processor (writing)—That processing component of writing that deals with correcting errors after a first draft has been written.

General task processor (reading)—That processing component of reading that controls for the general purpose of reading.

General task processor (writing)—That processing component of writing that deals with the general purpose for writing, the intended audience, and the adequacy of the writer's information base.

Graphemic processor (reading)—That component of reading that analyzes spelling patterns to aid in the recognition of words.

Graphemic processor (writing)—That processing component of writing that deals with the correct spelling of words.

Information Screener (reading)—That processing component of reading that judges the extent to which information appears reasonable.

Macrostructure generator (reading)—That processing component of reading that constructs a parsimonious representation of the information in the text.

Mediated instruction—The process of providing students with aid in specific skills they are developing while they are engaged in reading and writing.

Network processor (writing)—The processing component of writing that deals with the specific patterns of thought that have yet to be translated into sentences.

Parallel processing—Processing in which a number of interrelated components operate simultaneously while sharing information among themselves.

Project—A task that is partially specified, cognitively complex, student directed, and long-term in nature.

Proposition—The smallest unit of thought that can be affirmed or denied.

Propositional network processor (reading)—That processing component of reading that organizes ideas from sets of sentences into compact networks of ideas.

Sentence processor (writing)—That processing component of writing that translates networks of thoughts into coherent sentences.

Skills approach—An instructional philosophy that emphasizes learning specific reading and writing skills through drill and practice.

Superstructure—A large discourse pattern used to organize entire texts.

Whole-language approach—An instructional philosophy that emphasizes literacy development through holistic, meaningful reading and writing activities.

Word processor (reading)—The processing component of reading that deals with the recognition of words.

Word processor (writing)—The processing component of writing that deals with the appropriate selections of words to represent concepts within sentences.

Workshop—An instructional framework that involves a mini-lesson, an activity period, and a sharing period.

Zone of proximal development—The period during which a specific skill within a process such as reading or writing can be enhanced by focused help from a skilled adult.

References

Adams, M. J. (1990). *Beginning to read: Thinking and learning about reading. A summary*. Cambridge, MA: MIT Press.

Adams, M. J. (1992). Word recognition and reading. In C. J. Gordon, G. D. Labercane, & W. R. McEachern (Eds.), *Elementary reading instruction* (pp. 45–67). Needham Heights, MA: Ginn Press.

Anderson, J. (1990). *Cognitive psychology and its implications*. New York: Freeman.

Anderson, R. C., Hiebert, E. H., Scott, J. A., & Wilkinson, I. A. (1986). *Becoming a nation of readers*. Washington, DC: National Institute of Education.

Atwell, N. C. (1987). *In the middle*. Portsmouth, NH: Heinemann.

Balmuth, M. (1982). *The roots of phonics*. New York: Teachers College Press.

Bereiter, C., Fine, J., & Gartshore, S. (1979, March). *An exploratory study of microplanning in writing*. Paper presented at the annual meeting of the American Educational Research Association, San Francisco.

Bereiter, C., & Scardamalia, M. (1982). From conversation to composition: The role of instruction in a developmental process. In R. Glaser (Ed.), *Advances in instructional psychology* (Vol. 2, pp. 1–64). Hillsdale, NJ: Erlbaum.

Bereiter, C., & Scardamalia, M. (1985). Cognitive coping strategies and the problem of "inert knowledge." In S. F. Chipman, J. W. Segal, & R. Glaser (Eds.), *Thinking and learning skills*: Vol. 2. Research and open questions (pp. 65–80). Hillsdale, NJ: Erlbaum.

Bloom, A. (1987). *The closing of the American mind*. New York: Simon & Schuster.

Bradley, L. (1983). The organization of visual, phenological and motor strategies in learning to read and learning to spell. In U. Kirk (Ed.), *The neuropsychology of language, reading and spelling* (pp. 235–254). New York: Academic Press.

Britton, J. (1970). *Language and learning*. London: Penguin.

Britton, J. (1978). The functions of writing. In C. Cooper & L. Odell (Eds.), *Research on composing* (pp. 13–28). Urbana, IL: National Council of Teachers of English.

Brown, A. L., Campione, J. C., & Day, J. (1981, April). Learning to learn: On training students to learn from texts. *Educational Researcher*, 10, 14–24.

Brown, R. C. (1970). *Psycholinguistics*. New York: Macmillan.

Brown, R. C. (1973). *A first language*. Cambridge, MA: Harvard University Press.

Calkins, L. M. (1986). *The art of teaching writing*. Portsmouth, NH: Heinemann.

Chomsky, C. (1972). Stages in language development and reading exposure. *Harvard Educational Review*, 42, 1–33.

Clark, H. H., & Clark, E.V. (1977). *Psychology and language*. San Diego, CA: Harcourt Brace Jovanovich.

Clay, M. M. (1979). *The early detection of reading difficulties*. (3rd ed.). Birkenhead, Auckland, New Zealand: Heinemann Education.

Clay, M. M. (1991). *Becoming literate: The construction of inner control*. Portsmouth, NH: Heinemann.

D'Angelo, F. (1980). *Process and thought in composition* (2nd ed.). Cambridge, MA: Winthrop.

de Beaugrande, R. (1980). *Text, discourse and process: Toward a multi-disciplinary science of text*. Norwood, NJ: Ablex.

Feuerstein, R. (1980). Instrumental enrichment: An intervention program for cognitive modifiability. Baltimore: University Park Press.

Feuerstein, R., Rand, Y., Hoffman, M. B., & Miller, R. (1980). *Instrumental enrichment*. Baltimore, MD: University Park Press.

Flesch, R. (1955). *Why Johnny can't read*. New York: Harper & Row.

Flesch, R. (1981). *Why Johnny still can't read*. New York: Harper & Row.

Flower, L. A., & Hayes, J. R. (1980a). The cognition of discovery, defining a rhetorical problem. *College Composition and Communication*, 13, 21–32.

Flower, L. A., & Hayes, J. R. (1980b). The dynamics of composing: Making plans and juggling constraints. In L. W. Gregg & E. R. Steinburg (Eds.), *Cognitive processing in writing* (pp. 31–50). Hillsdale, NJ: Erlbaum.

Flower, L. A., & Hayes, J. R. (1981a). A cognitive process theory of writing. *College Composition and Communication*, 32, 365–387.

Flower, L. A., & Hayes, J. R. (1981b). Plans that guide the composing process. In C. H. Frederiksen & J. F. Dominic (Eds.), *Writing: The nature, development, and teaching of written communication* (Vol. 2, pp. 39–58). Hillsdale, NJ: Erlbaum.

Gazzaniga, M. S. (1985). *The social brain*. New York: Basic books.

Goodman, K. S. (1967, February). *Reading: A psycholinguistic guessing game*. Paper presented at the annual meeting of the American Educational Research Association. New York.

Goodman, K. S. (1986). *What's a whole in whole language?* Portsmouth, NH: Heinemann.

Gough, P. B. (1972). One second of reading. In J. F. Kavana & I. G. Mattingly (Eds.), *Language by ear and by eye* (pp. 331–358). Cambridge, MA: MIT Press.

Graves, D. (1983). *Writing: Teachers and children at work*. Portsmouth, NH: Heinemann.

Hansen, J. (1987). *When writers read*. Portsmouth, NH: Heinemann.

Hansen, J., & Graves, D. H. (1992). Unifying the English language arts curriculum. In J. Flood, J. M. Jensen, D. Lapp, & R. Squires, Jr. (Eds.), *Handbook of research on teaching the English language arts* (pp. 805–819). New York: Macmillan.

Hayes, J. R. (1981). *The complete problem solver.* Philadelphia: Franklin Institute.

Hayes, J. R., & Flower, L. S. (1980). Writing as problem solving. *Visible Language, 14,* 388–399.

Hillocks, G. (1986). *Research on written composition.* Urbana, IL: ERIC Clearinghouse on Reading and Communication Skills and National Conference on Research in English.

Hillocks, G. (1987). Synthesis of research in teaching writing. *Educational Leadership, 44*(8), 71–82.

Hirsch, E. D., Jr. (1987). *Cultural literacy: What every American needs to know.* Boston, MA: Houghton Mifflin.

Huey, E. B. (1915, 1974). *The psychology and pedagogy of reading.* Boston, MA: MIT Press.

Johnson-Laird, P. N. (1983). *Mental models.* Cambridge, MA: Harvard University Press.

Just, M. A., & Carpenter, P. A. (1987). *The psychology of reading and language comprehension.* Newton, MA: Alyn & Bacon.

Kearns, D. T. (1985). Forward. In A. N. Applebee, J. A. Langer, & I. V. S. Mullis (Eds.), *The nations report card: Learning to be literate in America* (pp. 1–5). Princeton, NJ: Educational Testing Service.

Kintsch, W. (1974). *The representation of meaning in memory.* Hillsdale, NJ: Erlbaum.

Kintsch, W. (1979). On modeling comprehension. *Educational Psychologist*, 1, 3–14.

Kintsch, W., & van Dijk, T. A. (1978). Toward a model of text comprehension and production. *Psychological Review*, 85, 363–394.

Klausmeier, H. J. (1980). *Learning and teaching concepts.* New York: Academic Press.

Kosslyn, S. M. (1980). *Image and mind.* Cambridge, MA: Harvard University Press.

LaBerge, D., & Samuels, S. J. (1976). Toward a theory of automatic information processing in reading. In H. Singer & R. B. Riddell (Eds.), *Theoretical models and processes of reading* (pp. 548–579). Newark, DE: International Reading Association.

Marzano, R. J. (1992). *A different kind of classroom.* Alexandria, VA: Association for Supervision and Curriculum Development.

Marzano, R. J. (1993). Toward a theory-based review of research on vocabulary. In C. J. Gordon, G. D. Labercane, & W. R. McEachern (Eds.), *Elementary reading process and practice* (2nd ed., pp. 29–44). Needham Heights, MA: Ginn.

Marzano, R. J., Haggerty, P. J., Valencia, S. W., & DiStefano, P. P. (1987). *Reading diagnosis and instruction: Theory into practice.* Englewood Cliffs, NJ: Prentice-Hall.

Marzano, R. J., & Marzano, J. S. (1988). *A cluster approach to elementary vocabulary instruction.* Newark, DE: International Reading Association.

Matsuhashi, A. (1981). Pausing and planning: The tempo of written discourse production. *Research in the Teaching of English*, 15, 113–134.

McNeil, J. D. (1984). *Reading comprehension: New directions for classroom practice.* Glenview, IL: Scott, Foresman.

Millword, C., & Bowie, L. (1980). *Workbook for writers.* New York: Holt, Rhinehart & Winston.

Mullis, I. V. S., Owen, E. H., & Phillips, G. W. (1990). *America's challenge: Accelerating academic achievement.* Princeton, NJ. Educational Testing Service.

Nagy, W. E. (1988). *Teaching vocabulary to improve reading comprehension.* Newark, DE: International Reading Association.

Nagy, W. E., & Anderson, R. C. (1984). How many words are there in printed school English? *Reading Research Quarterly,* 19, 303–330.

Nagy, W. E., Anderson, R. C., & Herman, P. A. (1987). Learning word meanings from context during normal reading. *American Education Research Journal,* 24, 237–270.

Nagy, W. E., & Herman, P. A. (1987). Breadth and depth of vocabulary knowledge. Implications for acquisition and instruction. In M. McKeown & M. Curtis (Eds.), *The nature of vocabulary instruction* (pp. 19–35). Hillsdale, NJ: Erlbaum.

Nagy, W. E., Herman, P. A., & Anderson, R. C. (1985). Learning words from context. *Reading Research Quarterly,* 20, 233–253.

Pearson, P. D., & Stephens, D. (1992). Learning about literacy: A 30–year journey. In C. J. Gordon, G. D. Labercane, & W. R. McEachern (Eds.), *Elementary reading instruction* (pp. 4–18). Needham Heights, MA: Ginn Press.

Pulliam, J. D. (1987). *History of education in America* (4th ed.). Columbus, OH: Merrill.

Shaughnessy, M. P. (1977). *Errors and expectations.* New York: Oxford University Press.

Smith, E. E., & Medin, D. L. (1981). *Categories and concepts.* Cambridge, MA: Harvard University Press.

Smith, F. (1982). *Understanding reading.* New York: Holt, Rhinehart & Winston.

Toulmin, S. (1958). *The uses of argument.* Cambridge, MA: Cambridge University Press.

Toulmin, S., Rieke, R., & Janik, A. (1981). *An introduction to reasoning.* New York: Macmillan.

Turner, A., & Greene, E. (1977). *The construction of a propositional text base.* Boulder, CO: Institute for the Study of Intellectual Behavior, University of Colorado at Boulder.

van Dijk, T. A. (1977). *Text and context.* London: Longman.

van Dijk, T. A. (1980). *Macrostructures.* Hillsdale, NJ: Erlbaum.

van Dijk, T., & Kintsch, W. (1983). *Strategies of discourse comprehension.* Hillsdale, NJ: Erlbaum.

Vygotsky, L. S. (1962). *Thought and language.* Cambridge, MA: MIT Press.

ABOUT THE AUTHORS

Robert J. Marzano, PhD, is Senior Program Director at the Mid-Continent Regional Educational Laboratory in Aurora, Colorado. His doctorate is in Educational Curriculum and Instruction from the University of Washington in Seattle. Over the past 20 years, he has specialized in translating research and theory in cognitive psychology into instructional techniques that can be used in grades K–12 across a variety of content areas.

Diane E. Paynter, a highly experienced classroom teacher, is now a Senior Program Associate at McREL. A nationally recognized speaker and trainer, she works extensively with teachers in the classroom, providing technical assistance and training in the areas of thinking skills and the integration of the language arts.